Companion to the Standing Stones

PROFILES OF NOTABLE PEOPLE FROM KEITH AND DISTRICT

Published by
Keith & District Heritage Group
www.kadhg.org.uk

PUBLISHED BY
KEITH & DISTRICT HERITAGE GROUP
SCOTTISH CHARITY NUMBER SCO33492

© KEITH & DISTRICT HERITAGE GROUP 2013

ISBN 978-0-9539787-6-2

COVER BY JOHN TASKER, DRYBRIDGE, BUCKIE

PRINTED BY MMS ALMAC, ISLA BANK MILLS, KEITH

ACKNOWLEDGEMENTS

Keith & District Heritage Group are greatly indebted to:

KEITH & STRATHISLA REGENERATION PARTNERSHIP (KSRP)
for help in funding the publishing of this book.

PETER LAING, Deputy Lord Lieutenant of Banffshire (Rtd)

THE BANFFSHIRE ADVERTISER

THE BANFFSHIRE HERALD

THE BANFFSHIRE JOURNAL

THE NORTHERN SCOT

THE PRESS & JOURNAL

THE MORAY COUNCIL LOCAL HERITAGE CENTRE STAFF

THE KEITH LIBRARY STAFF

BACK COVER: HYDE PARK, A PAINTING BY VERONICA MILNE

We are grateful to the many who have allowed us to use their photographs, especially:

> JUNE CAIRNS, HUGH EDGAR, SID KERR, CLUNY MACPHERSON, DAVID MCWILLIAM
>
> DESKTOP PUBLISHING BY DAVID MCWILLIAM

KEITH & DISTRICT HERITAGE GROUP MEMBERS for their help and support

The following contributors of articles are acknowledged under individual titles:
ALAN ANDERSON, MURIEL GRAY, DUNCAN MCKELVIE, MARY ROCHE, CHARLIE SIMPSON, RON SMITH.

FOREWORD
by
Peter Laing
Deputy Lord Lieutenant of Banffshire (Rtd)

The five parishes of Boharm, Botriphnie, Grange, Keith and Rothiemay together make up the central portion of Historic Banffshire. Therefore, when I was asked to write the Foreword for this collection of short biographies of memorable people from our area, I thought that, as a native of the parish of Keith, I would be quite familiar with their names. However, I was truly amazed at the number of people so worthy of inclusion and to learn of their wide and varied range of achievements.

Many have ventured forth from these shores to the far flung reaches of Empire and beyond in search of fame and fortune. Others have rarely strayed beyond the confines of their native parish. Some have come from afar to settle in the fertile lands of Strath Isla.

All have made significant contributions in their own particular field, from business and administration to academia, literature and sport. Others have served their country with great distinction and valour and have received military and civilian honours.
The members of Keith & District Heritage Group are to be congratulated on their tremendous achievement of drawing together all the names and full information of these remarkable individuals. They have succeeded in putting this into a book that makes excellent reading.

INTRODUCTION
by
Isobel Shanks
Heritage Group Co-ordinator

In June 2007 Keith & District Heritage Group erected three large monoliths in Scotscraig Gardens. On each of these Standing Stones there was a commemorative plaque listing the names of notable people from Keith and the surrounding parishes.

Later it became apparent that there were other names which could be added to the list. The Group therefore decided that a book should be produced to provide more details of the exploits and achievements of those people.

Heritage Group members **June Cairns, Joey Law and Isobel Shanks** embarked on the task of researching and writing these profiles. During their researches the team discovered even more names which they felt were worthy of inclusion.

It was decided to make use of the Group's extensive archive of historic photographic material in order to illustrate the articles. In addition, new photographs were taken to set the profiles in the local landscape. Finally, in 2013, the collection of life stories of these remarkable people from the area has been brought together in this book,

'COMPANION TO THE STANDING STONES'.

**Standing Stones in Scotscraig Gardens
and commemorative plaques**

6

CONTENTS

CONTENTS

CONTENTS

JAMES GORDON BENNETT, SENIOR
1792 – 1872

James Gordon Bennett, Senior, was born at Enzie in 1792, son of a poor crofter and, while still an infant, his family moved to Newmill near Keith.

James was educated at school in Newmill by teacher, Donald Cameron, and at Keith by the Rev. John Murdoch and was an able scholar. Upon finishing his education, he went to a Seminary in Aberdeen, then continued his studies in Spain. It was there he decided that he did not have a vocation for the priesthood.

James returned to Newmill and started work in Keith with Robert Stronach, a haberdasher. Later he went into business with his uncle, Cosmo Reid, in Aberdeen and this lasted for a number of years.

In 1819, along with his friend James Wilson from Keith, he decided to emigrate and, with only five pounds in his pocket, left for Halifax, Nova Scotia. He had some knowledge of Spanish, French and bookkeeping and so managed to support himself for a time. He moved to Boston in 1820 and there found employment as a proof reader, bookseller and translator. In 1823 he moved to New York and drifted into a variety of jobs, including freelance writer and editorial assistant on a newspaper. Finally he had found his forte and entered the newspaper business.

Spurred on with this type of work, he set up his own newspaper 'The New York Herald' in 1835. Initially he was editor, publisher and vendor. The paper recorded interesting and risqué facts in a brief form; it had no political allegiance and cost only one cent! He was the first to introduce the cash-in-advance method for advertising, which became the standard procedure for the industry. 'The New York Herald' was an instant success.

He had always contributed towards the welfare of his family back home and, on one occasion, was able to visit them in Newmill and Keith. It was noted that James helped and supported anyone from Banffshire he met in America.

He erected a gravestone in memory of his parents in the old cemetery in Keith and his daughter Jeannette (Mrs Isaac Bell) was later interred in the same grave.

James Gordon Bennett, Senior, died on 2nd June 1872, a self-made millionaire from Newmill, Keith.

Chapel at Kempcairn where James worshipped as a child

James at work in New York cellar

James Gordon Bennett senior

Announcement of President Lincoln's assassination in 1865

THE BENNETT CHILDREN
1841 - 1936

At a fashionable party in New York, James Gordon Bennett met and fell in love with a striking 21 year old music teacher, Henrietta Crean. She was a recent immigrant from Dublin where her grandfather, Nathaniel Warren, had been Lord Mayor 1782-83. James and Henrietta were married in New York in 1840.

J.G. Bennett Jnr

Their first child, James (or Jamie as his father called him), was born in 1841. Two further children, Cosmo (1844-1850) and Clementine (1847-1848), followed before their daughter Jeannette arrived in 1854.

Fearing for the safety of his family in the hostile social environment of New York, Bennett Snr sent his wife and family to Paris to live. When James Jnr's education was finished he returned to New York to learn from his father how to manage a newspaper empire. James Snr died in New York in 1872 and Henrietta passed away less than a year later in Koenigstein in Saxony.

After his father's death James Jnr took over the running of the New York Herald. His love of Paris and the European life-style, however, prevailed. He returned to France, established 'The International Herald Tribune' and then continued to manage both newspapers from Paris.

Bennett Jnr was a colourful, often eccentric, character and a keen sportsman. Like his father, he was an enterprising and innovative newspaper proprietor. He co-founded the transatlantic Commercial Cable Company, established the James Gordon Bennett Cup for international yacht races and other trophies

New York Herald Building

for aircraft, balloon and motor racing. Bennett funded the Henry Morton Stanley expedition to Africa to find David Livingstone, the Scottish explorer.

The saying "Gordon Bennett!", used as an expletive of shock, is said to have come about because of, at times, his quite scandalous and outrageous behaviour.

In 1878 he purchased the British gunboat, Pandora, refitted her and renamed her after his sister Jeannette. That year Jeanette had married a cotton broker, Isaac Bell (the thirteenth Isaac Bell in a line since the first one left Edinburgh for the Americas in 1640). The USS Jeannette, financed by Bennett and crewed by the Navy Department, set sail from San Francisco in 1879 for the Bering Strait. The 'Jeannette Expedition' was destined to enter the tragic annals of Arctic exploration. Beset by sea-ice the ship drifted helplessly for more than a year before sighting land which they named Jeannette Island. Formal possession of Jeannette Island, along with Henrietta Island, was proclaimed in the name of the American Government on 3rd June 1881. Bennett Island was discovered shortly afterwards adding to the United States' Siberian Islands territories. Tragedy struck when the USS Jeannette was crushed by the sea-ice, sank and most of the crew perished trying to reach the coast of Siberia.

US Navy Yacht Ensign

SY Jeannette at Le Havre 1878

Bennett Snr had once declined the offer by President Lincoln of the position of American Minister to France. His son-in-law, Isaac Bell, however, did accept the position of United States Minister to the Netherlands at The Hague from 1885 to 1888. After her husband's death in 1889 Jeannette lived mainly in Paris and also in England. She died in London in 1936. Jeannette had expressed the wish to be buried in Keith along with her grandparents, James Bennett who died in Newmill in 1824, and Janet Reid who died in Cuthil Street, Keith in 1854 aged 92. Her aunts Ann and Margaret are also buried here.

In 1916 the Russian Government stated their claim to the American Siberian islands of 1881. The United States never contested Russian or Soviet sovereignty of these islands.

James Jnr married late in life, at the age of 73, to Maud Potter, the widow of George, Baron de Reuter of the Reuter News Agency. On the 10th May 1918, James Gordon Bennett died; truly the end of an era!

Recently, some American politicians have tried, in the light of oil riches under the Arctic Ocean, to reopen the Jeannette Island sovereignty debate, so far with little success. Perhaps some day, in an energy-hungry future, the name of Jeannette, who rests peacefully in the Old Cemetery of Keith, will be even more well-known than those of her notorious brother or even her famous father.

Photo # NH 92127 "Jeannette Island", discovered by USS Jeannette north of Siberia, May 1881

Jeannette Island. From a Sketch by Mr. Melville.   **U.S. Flag**

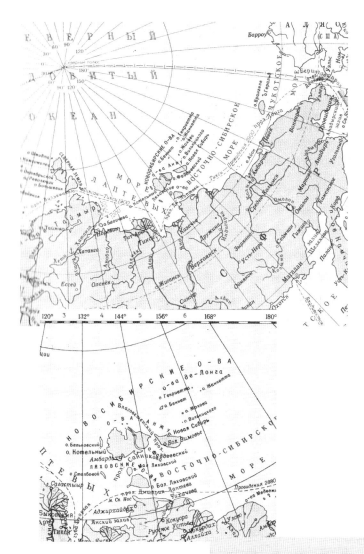

**Maps showing the Jeannette Expedition
Islands of 1879 - 1881**

Russian Imperial Flag

Jeannette Island

JAMES BRUCE
c 1840 - 1910

James Bruce, born c1840 in the Cabrach, was the son of James Bruce, blacksmith and general merchant, and Jane (nee Stewart). He was educated at the Cabrach Parish School and followed in his father's footsteps as a blacksmith. On his father's death he took over the running of the businesses.

Bailie James Bruce

About 1887 he moved to Keith and, having acquired the Brewery in Union Street (now part of Union Court), carried on a very successful business producing superior ale and aerated waters. The business included a bar serving ale and porter.

Mr Bruce served conscientiously on the Parochial Board and later on the Parish Council. In 1889, when Keith became a Police Burgh, Mr Bruce was a popular and successful candidate for the Town Council. In 1891 he topped the municipal poll. Three years later, he lost his seat but the following year was again successful and stayed in office until his death in 1910; in all, giving 20 years loyal service.

Mr Bruce had, as had many local prominent men of that time, a keen interest in the welfare of the people and of improving the amenities of the town. It was while he was a Junior Bailie, that he was responsible for the creation of the Steppies, previously known as the Stroupie Brae or Begg's Brae (between Turner Memorial Hospital and the Auld Toon). As a mark of their gratitude, the public presented him with a suitably-inscribed gold watch.

Bailie Bruce died a bachelor on 28th June 1910, and was buried in the Cabrach Churchyard. As a mark of esteem and respect, the Keith magistrates in attendance wore their robes of office.

The Steppies in winter

**An aerial view of the Auld Toon showing the site of
Bailie Bruce's Brewery on the corner of Union Street
behind the old Grammar School.**

GEORGE CLARK
1907-1986
Contributed by Charlie Simpson

Picture the scene, the year is 1951, and a crowded arena at the world famous Braemar Gathering has just witnessed a feat which hasn't been achieved since 1881. The massive Braemar caber, 19ft 3 ins in length, and weighing 120lbs, has just been tossed by a 44 year old Games veteran. It shouldn't have been too much of a surprise though, as the athlete in question was none other than the legendary George Clark of Grange. For this prodigious demonstration of strength and skill, the big man received special congratulations from the King and Queen, and from the organising committee a £10 award. Years later, the feat earned 'Big Geordie' a mention in the Guinness Book of Records.

Clark was born on 1st February 1907 at North Whiteley, Keith, and was brought up at Fortrie, Grange, as part of a large farming family. As a teenager he learned the art and craft of throwing the different weights and hammers with awesome power. Growing up on the farm, the young lads would stop for dinner and spent most of the hour throwing the hammer about. In the evenings they would be back at it again, hurling the hammer and the stone.

He was only 17 years old when he started competing on the Highland Games Circuit in 1924, and at his mightiest, was a fearsome 6ft 1 in, weighing a burly 17 stones, and had a chest expansion of around 50 inches.

He broke records with monotonous regularity competing against other Games powerhouses like Ed Anderson, Henry Gray and Jock McLellan. He had no peer for the best part of 30 years, holding the record for throwing the 56lb weight at Aboyne for over three decades, a distance of 39ft 6 ins. He also tossed the 28lb weight an amazing 76ft 4ins in 1934, a truly incredible distance.

The big man also excelled in Cumberland wrestling and took a liking to professional catch-as-catch-can wrestling , touring the United States, Canada and South Africa in the 1930's. In 1938 he twice fought reigning World Champion Lou Thesz in Hartford, Connecticut, losing on both occasions, but giving his all nevertheless. He did have the great distinction of defeating former world champion Danno O'Mahoney in Boston.

Larger than life Clark continued competing on the Games circuit well into his 50's, pitting himself against the likes of Arthur Rowe, Bill Anderson and Charlie Allan, winning prizes in the face of competition from athletes, many of whom were 30 years his junior.

Upon his retiral from active competition, he continued on the circuit as a judge, and his knowledge and experience were unsurpassed.

One of his last public appearances was at the revived Grange Games in 1986 where he was invited back as guest of honour. He died later that year in Torphins on 31st December just a month away from his 80th birthday.

Because of his pawky sense of humour he perhaps wasn't always the most popular athlete on the Games scene – but love him or hate him, one thing is certain – when the mighty men of the Scottish Highland Games are discussed, the legend that was big George Clark, has his name mentioned in the same breath as the marvellous Donald Dinnie, and A.A. Cameron as well as Bill Anderson. Yes, he was indeed that good!

George Clark at the Aboyne Games in the late 1950's

George Clark tossing the caber

SIR GEORGE CURRIE
1896 – 1984

George Alexander Currie was born on 13th August 1896 at Windyhills, Grange, son of George and Mary (nee Craib). He attended Crossroads School, Grange and Keith Grammar School. After serving in World War I with the Gordon Highlanders, George studied at Aberdeen University, graduating BSc.

He emigrated to Australia in 1923 and worked in tropical agriculture and cotton entomology in Queensland, before joining the staff at the Council for Scientific and Industrial Research. In 1936 he was awarded a DSc by Aberdeen University.

His career took him to Canberra, and in 1939, he accepted the appointment as Professor of Agriculture at the University of Western Australia, Perth, later becoming Principal and Vice Chancellor. While Vice Chancellor, he was involved in procuring the obsolete buildings used as living accommodation by American Navy personnel during World War II. The potential for the use of these buildings, which were adjacent to the University, as a hostel for the students was realised in 1946. In 1960 the hostel was named, 'Currie Hall'. Eventually the old hostel had to be replaced by more modern facilities which, to this day, still bear the name of, 'Currie Hall', a fitting tribute to a much respected Vice Chancellor.

In 1952, he was made Vice Chancellor of New Zealand University, specialising in agricultural research, later returning to Australia.

In 1960, he received a Knighthood. Degrees of LLD were conferred from the Universities of Aberdeen, Melbourne, Dalhousie (Canada) and New Zealand, and from Western Australia a DLitt, with a further LLD from Papua New Guinea. He retired to Canberra, and died there on 3rd May 1984.

Currie Cocksfoot
(Dactylis glomerata) -
developed from seed
collected by George
Currie in Algeria and
introduced to Australia
by him.

Crossroads School

THOMAS DICK
1872 - 1923

MARGARET DICK
1868 - 1944

Thomas Dick was born on 1st December 1872 at Dunphail, Elginshire. His father, James, was station master at Dunphail, and later at Grantown and at Edinkillie. The family then returned to Dunphail where his father took up the position of postmaster and grocer.

In 1883 the family of six daughters and three sons moved to Keith where James, the father, set up a grocery business at 45/47 Mid Street. In due course Thomas was apprenticed to his father and eventually took over the very successful business.

Thomas married Margaret Grant, daughter of a local blacksmith. Of the two other brothers, one went to Perth (Scotland) and the other to San Francisco. The six sisters married, and three of them lived locally.

Thomas and Margaret had no children. In 1923, Thomas, at the young age of 51, died in the Albyn Nursing Home, Aberdeen. Margaret sold the business which continued under a succession of owners, viz: Messrs Fraser, Leslie, Spiers, Smith and Petrie for another 50 years.

Thomas and Margaret Dick did not forget their Keith roots and set up a bequest in Margaret's Will, 'The Thomas and Margaret Dick Fund'. Once a year, at Christmas, Trustees allocate the income to members of St Rufus, the North and Newmill Churches who are over sixty years of age.

Thomas Dick's great grandfather, James Dick, was a community minded man. He resided in Elgin and his trade was that of a blacksmith. During that time he was Deacon of 'The Incorporation of Blacksmiths', and convener of 'The Incorporated Trades in Elgin'; Thomas would seem to have inherited his great grandfather's community spirit.

Dunphail Railway Station

Shop, previously owned by Thomas Dick, situated next to Malta House in Mid Street. Young apprentice grocers Alexander Lemmon and George Blackhall.

JOHN (JOCK) DUNBAR
1926 – 2007

John Dunbar was born in Keith on 9th March 1926, and lived with his family in Union Street. He received his education in Keith at the Green School and later at the Grammar School. On leaving school he began work with the London and North Eastern Railway.

At the age of 21, John decided to emigrate to Canada and found work with the Hudson Bay Mining and Smelting Company. He had always enjoyed singing and during his time with the Hudson Bay Company he entered his first singing competition – and won it! When he returned to work, the foreman gave him a job in the storeroom, in case the dust in the mine might damage his voice.

From there, he moved on to work in the ticket office of the Canadian Pacific Railway at Victoria, British Columbia. John continued training for his singing career, and gained a scholarship to the Metropolitan Opera School in New York. While there, he met Robert Wilson, the well known Scottish tenor, who was on tour in Canada. Robert persuaded John to return to Scotland and perform at the Gaiety Theatre, Ayr. With his wife, Joan, and his two small children, he travelled back to Scotland for the season. The move was a success and he received many offers of theatre work, and the BBC engaged him for a live broadcast on New Year's Eve. There followed regular performances on BBC Radio and Television and a recording contract with Pye Records.

The Dunbar family returned to Vancouver, Canada, for a 'one off' performance at the McPherson Theatre and decided to make Vancouver their base. After returning to Britain to honour a singing agreement, John was approached by Henry Hall, who wanted him to succeed Edmund Hockridge, a Canadian baritone, in a West End production. Although tempted, he declined the offer, and set sail for New York and home to Vancouver.

For the next thirty years his career flourished until his retirement, but even that didn't stop him from giving performances on special occasions. John returned to his hometown of Keith to visit his parents and siblings and, without fail, he would perform in St Rufus Church - the favourite being his rendition of 'The Lord's Prayer'. His final performance was at the 2005 Men's World Curling Championships in Victoria, British Columbia, where he sang 'Scotland the Brave' and 'Haste ye Back'.

John, or Jock as he was affectionately known worldwide, died in his adopted homeland of Canada on June 18th 2007.

**Singing at
'Stars of Tomorrow'**

Union Street where John grew up at No. 39

JAMES FERGUSON
1710 - 1776

James Ferguson, the famous astronomer and instrument maker, was born at Core of Mayen on the boundary of the parishes of Rothiemay and Marnoch and was baptised there on 25th April 1710. He was the second child of John Ferguson, a tenant farmer, and his wife, Elspet Lobban. When James was about two, the family moved to Keith and, at a later date, to Grange.

John Ferguson was keen that his sons should be literate and taught them himself to read and to write. James' formal education consisted of one term's attendance, when he was about seven years old, at the Parish school of Keith.

A delicate child, he was fee'd as a shepherd boy from the age of ten, first with neighbouring farmer, Alexander Middleton, and then with James Glashan of Ardneadlie (now a part of Braehead, just south of the town of Keith). They both indulged the boy in his early interest in mechanical models and astronomy. He would study the night sky and, by means of strings and beads, would map the constellations and draw his 'Star-papers'.

The Churchyard at Keith would be pivotal in the story of James Ferguson. Here he attended the School next to the Church for three months under schoolmaster John Skinner. It was also here that two chance, but fortuitous, encounters changed the course of his life. The first was with Alexander Cantly, butler to Thomas Grant of Auchoynanie, who was painting the sundial at the corner of the school building. The second was with Mr Grant himself, who was introduced to young James by the minister, the Rev. John Gilchrist. This resulted in a move to Auchoynanie under the patronage of Thomas Grant and being schooled by his polymath butler in arithmetic, algebra and geometry. Ferguson later described the self-taught Alexander Cantly as "the most extraordinary man that I ever was acquainted with" and as "God Almighty's scholar".

In 1730 butler Cantly moved from Auchoynanie to employment with William Duff of Braco (the owner of extensive estates in the North East and later to become Lord Braco and Earl Fife). This prompted Ferguson to leave Auchoynanie for pastures new.

School in the Churchyard

Ferguson 1756

Two disastrous periods of employment then befell young James. The first was when he was fee'd to the Mill of Tarnash for a year but was overworked and underfed by the miller who was 'too fond of tippling at an Ale-house'. The second was at Pitlurg where he was engaged by Dr Young , a local farmer and country physician, who agreed to give him instruction in medicine. However, the promised instruction never materialised and, after three months of 'very hard labour', Ferguson left 'the hardest Master... very weak and much emaciated'. His old friend and mentor, butler Cantly, re-appears in the story and comes to his erstwhile pupil's rescue by supplying the necessary medicines for Ferguson's lengthy recovery.

Alexander Cantly and his connections with the interlinked aristocratic families of the North East may have helpful in the next step of Ferguson's career. Duff of Braco's stepmother was Jean Duff (usually known as Lady Dipple) and it was at her brother's residence near Portsoy that Ferguson next found employment. Sir James Dunbar of Durn engaged him to clean and maintain the clocks at Durn House and to repair other pieces of equipment. Based at Durn House, Ferguson soon developed a clock-cleaning business among the landed families and big houses of the North East. It was here among the paintings at Durn that he discovered his artistic talents. Lady Dipple and others commissioned him to design embroidery patterns for needlework, which was all the fashion among the ladies of the aristocracy at the time.

The Dunbar connections spread far and wide around the established families of the North East. Jean Dunbar (Lady Dipple) was married into the increasingly powerful Duffs. Her sister Anne was the mother of James Ogilvy, later Earl of Findlater and Seafield, and founder of New Keith in 1750. Lady Dipple's daughter, Anne Duff, was married to William Baird of Auchmeddan. The large library at Auchmeddan House near Pennan was a great attraction for Ferguson, who spent eight months there absorbing as much as he could with Baird translating from Greek, Latin and French as required.

Auchoynanie

Mill of Tarnash

Lady Dipple

Ferguson's talent in copying the portraits and pictures at Durn and Auchmeddan so impressed Baird and Lady Dipple, that she took him to her house in Edinburgh with a view to setting him up in an apprenticeship as an artist. A letter of introduction from Alexander Forbes, Lord Pitsligo, to the Edinburgh artist John Alexander resulted in an offer of a seven-year unpaid position. Not unsurprisingly, the apprenticeship was not taken up.

Bishop Robert Keith, a friend of William Baird, then suggested that Ferguson would need no further professional instruction in order to embark on a career as a 'limner' or portrait artist. For the next two years he was based at the home of his patron, Lady Dipple, who introduced him to her friends and acquaintances in Edinburgh society. Among these were Lady Jane Douglas and her mother, the Marchioness of Douglas, of Merchiston Castle, where Ferguson was specially permitted to use the room in which Napier had devised his Logarithms.

During this successful and financially rewarding sojourn among the elite of the capital, Ferguson rekindled his ambition of becoming a doctor. He eagerly studied Anatomy, Surgery and Medicine - all from books - and, in 1736, returned North to Strathisla to practise as a country physician. Alas, he discovered that book learning was no substitute for experience, and the general poverty of his patients made for a poor financial return. Abandoning this particular career path, he then married nineteen year-old Isabel Wilson from Cantly in Grange and went to Inverness, there to resume his business as a portrait painter.

At Inverness he devised and computed his 'Astronomical Rotula', tables which predicted various astronomical events as far as the year 1800. This so impressed Colin Maclaurin, Professor of Mathematics and Natural Philosophy at Edinburgh University that he raised the money to have Ferguson print and publish them in 1742. After a brief return to Edinburgh, Ferguson and his wife set sail from Leith in May 1743 for London and new horizons.

Durn House

28

Carrying a letter of recommendation to the influential Stephen Poyntz in the Royal Court at St James, Ferguson soon established a successful portrait-painting business in London. He quickly made contact with Martin Folkes, the President of the Royal Society, who invited him to deliver a presentation to the Society on his latest work on the Moon's orbit, his 'trajectorium lunare'. In 1746 Ferguson tentatively published his first literary attempt, 'The Use of a New Orrery', the first of a long list of pamphlets and books on all aspects of experimental philosophy.

On 20th March 1746, he presented his paper, 'On the Phenomena of Venus', to the Royal Society. Little did he realise that, on that very night, in the Churchyard of Keith, where he had enjoyed his three months of formal education, and where he had first met his mentor and patron, Alexander Cantly and Thomas Grant of Auchoynanie, the last successful fling of the Jacobite Rebellion was taking place. The Skirmish of Keith was soon followed by the resounding defeat of the rebels at Culloden.

In 1748 Ferguson began his extremely successful career as a popular scientific teacher and lecturer, starting with lectures on the 1748 solar eclipse and then including many diverse branches of science, such as mechanics, hydrostatics, hydraulics, pneumatics and electricity. His popular and lucrative tours, in which he used models and machines to illustrate his lectures, took him to all the major cities in the country. His most successful work was published in 1756, 'Astronomy Explained Upon Sir Isaac Newton's Principles'. It went through thirteen editions and was translated into several languages.

He became a friend of George, Prince of Wales, later King George III, and received an annuity of £50 for life from the Privy Purse. In 1763 Ferguson was elected a Fellow of the Royal Society and in 1770 he received transatlantic recognition when elected a Fellow of the American Philosophical Society.

James Ferguson died in London on 16th November 1776 and was buried in the Churchyard of St Mary-le-bone.

"Astronomy and Mechanics he taught
with singular success and reputation.
He was modest, sober, humble, and religious,
and
His works will immortalize his memory,"

King George III

29

LEWIS W. FORBES
1794 - 1854

Lewis William Forbes was born in 1794, son of George Forbes, advocate in Aberdeen and Sheriff Substitute in Banff. Educated at Kings College in Aberdeen, he graduated Master of Arts in 1811.

He was licensed by the Presbytery of Forres in 1815 and was ordained as Church of Scotland Minister in Boharm in 1816. In 1821 the Boharm Parish Savings Bank was instituted under the management of the Minister.

In 1851 he graduated Doctor of Divinity at Marischal College, Aberdeen. The following year, Dr Forbes became Moderator of the General Assembly of the Church of Scotland, a great honour, as this is usually bestowed on a minister of an important city charge, not a quiet country parish. This speaks volumes for the high regard in which he was held.

Dr Forbes compiled the Boharm section of the 'New Statistical Account of Scotland - 1842'.

He married his first wife, Penelope Cowie, at Banff in 1816 and they had four sons and one daughter. Penelope died in September 1827.

On 20th October 1835, he married Elizabeth Mary Leslie at Kininvie and they had three sons and five daughters. One of their sons was Archibald Forbes. (See next entry.)

Rev. Dr Lewis W. Forbes died aged 60 on 8th January 1854 in the School House, Boharm and was buried in Boharm Cemetery.

Boharm Manse built 1811

30

Boharm Kirk

**Leaving nothing to chance
- a lucky horseshoe!**

PARISH OF BOHARM.

PRESBYTERY OF ABERLOUR, SYNOD OF MORAY.

THE REV. L. W. FORBES, A. M., MINISTER.

New Statistical Account of Scotland 1842

I.—TOPOGRAPHY AND NATURAL HISTORY.

In very early times, there seems to have been a parish of Arndilly, then called Artendol, the church of which stood on the eminence which is now the site of the mansion-house of Arndilly, on the banks of the Spey, in the south-west corner of the present parish. Vestiges of such ecclesiastical occupation of this lovely spot

31

ARCHIBALD FORBES
1838 – 1900

Archibald Forbes, born in 1838, was the son of Rev. Dr Lewis William Forbes and his second wife, Elizabeth Mary Leslie . (See previous entry.) He was a military historian and war correspondent, serving in many theatres of war, most important of those being the Zulu wars of 1879 to 1880.

Archibald was a generous minded man and was highly decorated by many governments. In short, a man who brought honour and fame to his native Boharm. He was also a writer of books, one being 'Memories of War and Peace'.

A portrait of Archibald Forbes with his medals still hangs in the Mulben Public Hall, a fitting tribute, as he generously bequeathed books to the library, which was later housed in the Hall.

He died in London in 1900 and is buried in Allenvale cemetery in Aberdeen. His wife, Louise, had a bronze tablet with a massive border of green marble erected to her husband's memory in Boharm Church. Above the inscription is a copy of the Iron Cross of Germany, a decoration conferred upon Archibald Forbes by the German Emperor at the time of the Franco Prussian War.

Looking over Boharm towards Ben Aigen

One of the most
decorated civilians
of all time.

Memorial Tablet

Archibald Forbes on various campaigns.

33

LT. COL. JOHN FOSTER FORBES
1835 – 1914

John Foster Forbes was born on 11th December 1835, the first child of Lieut. Col. John Forbes of the Bombay Army and his wife Eliza (nee Orrok). Educated at Edinburgh Military Academy, he saw service during the 1857-58 Indian Mutiny and commanded the 36th Indian Cavalry Regiment (Jacob's Horse). Lieut. Col. Forbes showed great bravery and leadership during his military career, and was twice wounded. He was mentioned twice in dispatches and recommended for the Victoria Cross for gallantry.

In 1873, he married Mary Livesey and they had seven sons and two daughters. All his sons were encouraged to join the army or navy, and those who fulfilled their father's wishes rose in the ranks to make him proud.

Lieut. Col. Forbes purchased Rothiemay Estate in 1890 and took up residence in 1894. He loved his castle and, being a skilled craftsman, made all his own furniture. The castle, estate and village of Rothiemay flourished under his patronage. He donated an improved water supply to the village and, in 1913, handed over the Public Hall to the parish. He served as a Justice of the Peace and Depute Lord Lieutenant for Banffshire.

He died at the family castle on 3rd November 1914.

Arms of the old Lairds of Rothiemay

Castle Gateway with Coat of Arms

Lt. Col. John Foster Forbes

Rothiemay Castle

MARY FORBES
1854 – 1929

Mary Livesey was born on 23rd September 1854, at Beach, Cheshire, and in 1873 married Lieut. Col. John F. Forbes. The Forbes family took up residence in Rothiemay Castle in 1894, having purchased the Estate in 1890.

Mrs Forbes took an active interest in the community, being a very able speaker and organiser. She channelled her enthusiasm into the newly formed Women's Rural Institute. She was the first President of the Rothiemay Branch, which, in 1917, was the second Branch to be registered in Scotland. She gave freely of her time to other interests, including missionary work, and the Rothiemay, Knock and Ordiquhill Nursing Association, and was an ardent worker for the National Council of Women.

In 1921 she opened the newly-built Rothiemay Hall, which replaced the original Hall burnt down in 1916.

On the death of her husband, she took over the Estate. Mary Forbes died in London on 29th April 1929 and the estate then passed to her eldest surviving son, Col. Ian Forbes, D.S.O.

Rothiemay Hall with decorative plaques from the old castle thought to depict History, Comedy and Tragedy

Mrs Mary Forbes

Rothiemay Castle

ISA FORREST
c1865 - 1937

Isa Forrest was a well-known local poet whose works frequently appeared in the local Keith and Strathisla weekly newspaper, 'The Banffshire Herald'.

Isa or Isabella was born about 1865 in the parish of Fordyce, the daughter of Robert Esson, a carter and salmon-fisher, and Elsphet Taylor. Isa lived with her grandmother, Isabella Esson, who was gatekeeper at Glassaugh House in Fordyce.

In 1890 Isa married James Forrest in Fordyce and the couple later lived in Grange and then at Lilac Neuk on the road from Keith to Mulben.

Isa's poems covered a wide range of subjects from idyllic descriptions of local beauty spots to the horrors of war in far-off lands. Many of her poems touched on the various social issues of the day such as class and wealth, improvement through education, women and the vote.

Local as well as national events featured in her poetry, often in the form of an address to some local dignitary or well-known character. A collection of her poems entitled 'Islaside Musings' was produced and printed by the Banffshire Journal.

Isa Forrest died at Lilac Neuk on 16th October 1937 and was buried in Broomhill Cemetery in Keith.

KNOCKDHU.

Ye Temperance Leaders, cease your strife,
Since whisky stills are growin' sae rife,
For even near the Knock Hill noo
Ye'll get the best o' "mountain dew."

If ye'd in moderation taste
It wadna hairm ye in the least;
Tae tak' a drap an' nae get fu'
For that just spoils the real Knockdhu.

The Land o' Edingicht

The wee Kirk at the hill-fit
Has mouldered to decay,
And a far mair spacious structure
Noo marks the place the day

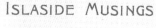

ISLASIDE MUSINGS

BY

ISA. FORREST
KEITH

PRINTED BY
THE BANFFSHIRE JOURNAL, LTD.,
BANFF.

At Lilac Neuk

THE SILENT WARRIOR.

The following lines were inspired, on "Remembrance Day," while paying homage at Keith War Memorial to the memory of those who sacrificed their lives in the Great War.

Silent warrior, vigil keeping
O'er our dear, beloved dead,
Sadly do we bow before thee,
Reverently unbare the head.

THE HYDE PARK TANNERY – THE FORSYTH FAMILY
c1727 - 1895
Contributed by Duncan McKelvie

The Hyde Park Tannery was founded in c1727 by James Forsyth, who was still working until the very day he died at the age of 90 years. The business was then carried on by his son, John, and subsequently, on John's death, it was passed to grandsons, Edward and John. Of the two, John Jnr was the academic one and gained a bursary to Marischal College in Aberdeen. Family circumstances, however, prevailed upon him and he returned home to share the responsibility of running the Tannery. It would seem that John Jnr left most of the managing of the works to Edward, as he preferred to take up a teaching post at Keith Public School. He also increased the scope of the business by starting up a Dye Works at nearby Earlsmill.

During his lifetime, John Jnr was a member of local and county boards and a founder member of 'The Domestic Friendly Society of Keith', which met in 'Skinner's Inn' at 69 Land Street.

Towards the end of the 19th century, as the new chemical processes for tanning were introduced and cheap bison hides from America flooded the market, the business slid into decline and so, around 1895, the life of the Tannery came to an end.

The booming railway industry had houses built for its workers alongside the defunct Tannery. By the end of the 20th century, changes in industrial practices, and the restructuring of the railway system, resulted in the Tannery and the railway houses being demolished.

John Forsyth Jnr was instrumental in the laying out of the 1870 extension to the old cemetery. Various members of the Forsyth Family also took it upon themselves to meet the responsibility and expense of maintaining the Auld Brig of Keith.

Keith Tannery at Hyde Park

Forsyth Family

Earlsmill

ALEXANDER & WILLIAM GARDEN
1845-1929   1848-1902

Alexander was born in 1845 and his brother William in 1848. They were born into a family of twelve children to James Garden, a limeworks carter and farmer, and his wife Margaret Main on a croft on Auchanacie Muir, two miles south-west of Keith. The brothers were gifted poets, and their contributions in their 'mither tongue' were descriptive of their way of life. They attended school at Auchanacie during the winter months but in the summer had to work as herd boys on the croft.

When Alexander left school he worked on local farms and later as a labourer on the railways in various parts of Scotland. At the age of nineteen he was inspired by Robert Burns and began to compose verse and had a number of poems published in newspapers and periodicals. In 1869 he entered the Edinburgh Police Force and the following year married Mary McDonald, originally from Glass. After a further spell of farm work and a second period of Police service he returned to railway work with the North British Railway Company at Berwick on Tweed. He was later a carter and coal agent in Edinburgh and died there in 1929.

Extract from 'THE PARISH O' KEITH' by Alexander

In lovely Strathisla I aince had a hame,
That stood by a hillside I min' weel the name;
A rude cottage biggit wi' stanes an' wi' clay,
Its tiggin was theckit wi' heather an' strae,
And here is my birthplace, I prood tae confess,
An; tell ye I think it an honour nae less:
Tho' the haughty may cast the same in my teeth,
I'm prood I belang tae the Parish o' Keith.

Robert Burns

William Donaldson

42

Upon leaving school, William also became a farm servant for a short time before training in the baking trade with Mrs Munro in Mid Street, Keith. In the evenings he attended a literary society where he met William Donaldson, a local poet, who published 'The Queen Martyr' in 1867. Inspired, William began to write poetry and in 1868 he published a very successful volume entitled 'Meg's Wedding and Other Poems'. He moved to Edinburgh for a short time as a journeyman baker before returning North to set up a business in Archiestown. He later moved to Newmill and finally to Inverness about 1894. William was married twice and died in Church Street, Inverness in 1902.

Extract from 'THE AULD MAN'S FAREWEEL' by William

In the cloudless blazin' mornin'
O' life's bricht happy hours,
When a' aroun' was smilin'
Like burstin' bloomin' flowers,
An' the birds a' sweetly chantin'
On ilka leafy tree,
Thy voice was aye the sweetest,
Like the saftly humin' bee.

View of Auchanacie Muir with Muldearie Hill in the background

ALEXANDER (SANDY) GARDEN MBE
1924 – 2006

Alexander (Sandy) Garden was born at Keith in June 1924 and educated at Keith Primary School (Green School) and Keith Grammar School. On leaving, he found employment with the Keith branch of the national grocery store, Lipton, which had premises on Mid Street. He then moved on to other Lipton Store outlets in Nairn, Oban and Fort William.

At the age of 18, with World War II in full progress, he was conscripted into the Army and had his basic military training at Fort George. When that training was complete, he was dispatched for further training with the Royal Signals at Catterick, in Yorkshire. From there he was sent, as a wireless operator, to join the 38th Welsh Infantry Divisional Headquarters. Mr Garden spent several months there, before moving to Henley-on-Thames to receive specialised training in clandestine operations, and to become a member of the elite Special Operations Executive (SOE).

He was posted to India, to join Force 136, which was based in Calcutta. Here, he was involved in many secret operations, until a bout of malaria temporarily stopped his operational movements. When the war ended in 1945, he was still in the Far East, and Force 136 was no longer required, so the unit was made responsible for communications for RAPWI (Recovery of Allied Prisoners of War and Internees). When this, too, came to an end, Force 136 was disbanded and Mr Garden was posted back to the regular army.

On his return to Britain he was assigned to the Signals HQ at Pocklington, Yorkshire, and finished his Army career as a clerk in the demobilisation department of the Royal Signals.

After his own demobilisation, Mr Garden returned to Keith and then enrolled in the Leith Nautical College. Upon graduating, he joined the Foreign Office as a communications officer.

For the next 34 years he worked all over the world; Britain, Finland, Pakistan, Cyprus, China, Ascension Island, Malaysia and Saudi Arabia.

In 1982 he received an MBE from the Queen at Buckingham Palace in recognition of his work, although Mr. Garden never revealed why he had been given the Honour.

The following year he retired to Keith and integrated into his home community. He was a founder member, and past office bearer, of the Keith Probus Club and a member of the Keith District Branch of the Royal British Legion, and always took part in the Remembrance Day Service. He was also an elder of St Rufus

Church. Mr Garden remained a bachelor and had a close relationship with his Keith nieces and nephews, plus their extended families. He died on 17th November 2006 and was buried in Broomhill Cemetery, Keith.

Force 136 was set up by Prime Minister Winston Churchill as a wartime surveillance unit to link up with the Resistance movements in occupied countries. Therefore, was Mr Garden, a Keith lad, an undercover agent? We will never know - he took his secret to his grave in 2006.

MBE

ALEXANDER STRUTHERS GEORGE
1815 – 1892

Alexander Struthers George was born on 26th March 1815, the son of James George, of Haughs, Keith, and Jane (nee Littlejohn). It was his ambition to become a solicitor and he served as an apprentice with a lawyer in Glasgow.

He returned North to Portsoy, where he had a fish curing business, and later joined his brother John, to take over their late father's wheat and flour business at 'Mills of Keith'. It is reported that Alexander George would create work in harsh winters in order to provide income for his men.

He was Vice President on the Board of Directors of Turner Memorial Hospital and it was he who officially opened the building on 31st December 1880.   He was also Chairman of the Board of Directors of the Institute and represented the Public Library.

Among other posts held were; Chairman of Keith Parochial Board, Sheriff Substitute and Justice of the Peace. He was also a keen supporter of Keith Bowling Club.

Alexander and his wife Mary (nee Christall) had fourteen children – five sons and nine daughters. His wife, Mary, opened the new Glacks of Balloch water supply for the town of Keith in 1879.

 The family moved from Keith to Dublin, then Brighton and finally London, where he died on 17th January 1892, and was interred in the old Kirkyard of Keith.

Mills of Keith (now Glen Keith Distillery)

Linn of Keith showing Mill of Keith and its lade

Turner Memorial Hospital

**Earlsmount,
the George Family home**

Keith Institute

DUNCAN GILLIES
1953 –
Contributed by Charlie Simpson

Imagine you are at a typical Scottish Highland Games.......The skirl o' the bagpipes, the Highland dancers treading the boards, the Heavies birling the weights and tossing the cabers, straining every sinew in the process. Then, the P.A. system crackles, and resounding around the crowded arena you hear "And first into the park from the Hill Race is Duncan Gillies from Keith".

For a spell, from about 1974-75 to 1991-92, that sentence was uttered by commentators the length and breadth of Scotland and beyond. "Gillies of Keith" was a name that struck fear into the hearts of the very best British professional hill and fell runners during that period. He won races, championships, cups and medals by the hatful, breaking records in the most astonishing manner.

Hawkswick Dash in Yorkshire

Duncan was born on 8th March 1953 in Turner Memorial Hospital, Keith and was brought up at Muiryfold, Grange. It should have been no real surprise that he would excel at hill running, then latterly at cycling, as the large Gillies family, his father and uncles, were all notable runners, walkers and cyclists in their day.

Locally, he made the Knock Hill Race, Cornhill his own, winning it 12 times, including a remarkable 11 successive times from 1977-87. He still holds the record time of 52 minutes 24 seconds for the eight and a half mile course, which includes the ascent and descent of the 1,406 foot high Hill.

However, it was further afield that he made a more telling impression. At his peak, he was quite simply a supreme competitor. One of his finest moments came in 1984, by this time living at Aultmore outside Keith, when he clinched the Holy Grail of British professional hill racing, the British Championships. He became the first ever Scotsman to win, down at Alva Games, Stirlingshire, in front of a crowd of well over 5,000, pipping reigning champion Steve Carr of Kendal on the line.

He achieved legendary status the following year, daring to win the Blue Riband of English fell running at Grassmere in the Lake District. He was a 20-1 outsider but in front of 10,000 spectators he gained revenge for losing his British title earlier in the year by snatching victory from Carr. That made him the first ever Scot to win the English title in the

Race's 133 year history. 'The Wee Highlander' his English counterparts dubbed him, but the likes of Carr, Graham Moffat and the legendary Fred Reeves all respected him hugely.

Uniquely, in 1980, he achieved the triple 'Deeside Games'– Braemar, Ballater and Aboyne Hill races, a feat no-one has ever equalled.

He turned briefly to Triathlons, before extending his expertise to purely cycling and joined Elgin Cycling Club, where he proceeded to rewrite their record books for distances over 10 miles – 22mins 15 seconds, 25 miles – 55mins 39 seconds, 30 miles, 50 miles – 1 hour 55 mins 53 seconds and 100 miles – 4hours 26 mins 33 seconds. In 1991, he returned to Alva, the scene of his British Hill running triumph to win the Scottish 2 miles grass track cycling championships, a truly unique double!

Cyclists half his age regularly fell by the wayside capitulating to the prowess and steely determination of an athlete, who simply had no right to be winning races and posting times that blew them away. Indeed, at the Elgin Club he was Club Cyclist of the Year eight years on the trot, had a year off, then was crowned the following year for a ninth time.

The most unassuming of characters, humble in his exploits, he was a real 'Alf Tupper – Tough of the Track' character who was proud of his roots. He competed with the greatest of distinction and is rightly revered in the annals of hill and fell running.

**Ambleside,
Lake District**

**Duncan with his
cups and trophies**

49

JAMES GOODALL
c1902 - 1936

James Goodall was an Aberdeen man, but bought a garage business in Moss Street, Keith in the early 1930s with the money from winning a bet on the Derby horse race. He was interested in aviation and had an ambition to build his own aircraft.

About this time a Frenchman, Henri Mignet, designed a home-built craft called 'Pou du Ciel', which translates as Sky Louse, but became popular in Britain as the 'Flying Flea'. Mignet claimed that any man who could nail the lid on a packing case could construct his own aeroplane, and that the man in the street could make one for about £70. At this time there was no legislation controlling home-built aircraft. The number of 'Fleas' being built in Britain, and the number of fatalities which resulted, caused the Air Ministry to introduce legislation in the form of a Permit to Fly.

James decided to build one in his garage, with the assistance of other local men. An engineer named Stewart built the laminated propeller, and Eddie Herd, a local jeweller, made a curved windscreen from Perspex and aluminium. The plane was powered by a Douglas motor cycle engine.

The aircraft was completed in 1936 and was registered as G-ADXY. With no previous experience, or training, James carried out a successful test flight from the airfield at Dyce. The plane initially appeared to be a success but, on a later flight at Dyce, he crashed and died from his injuries in Foresterhill Hospital.

Crashes of 'Fleas' and the deaths of their pilots became too frequent and eventually legislation was passed banning their use.

James Goodall may not have originated in Keith, but, for a time, he brought great interest to his adopted place of residence.

James Goodall with his Flying Flea

James Goodall's mother 'tests' the Flying Flea

DR. ISABELLA GORDON
1901 - 1988

Isabella Gordon was born in Keith on 18th May 1901 at 39 Back Street, (now called Balloch Road), the only daughter of James Gordon and Margaret, nee Lamb. Her brothers, John and James, later completed the family. She was educated at Keith Primary School and Keith Grammar School, where she received an £8 annual bursary for three years which enabled her to continue school until 17 years of age.

In 1918 she furthered her education at Aberdeen University and became a student demonstrator in practical zoology. After having qualified as a primary and science teacher at the Aberdeen Teacher Training College, Isabella continued her studies at Aberdeen University. She received the first Kilgour Research Scholarship and graduated BSc Hons in 1922.

In 1924 she had two publications to her credit. The following two years were spent studying at the Imperial College of Science at the University of London, where she graduated with a PhD degree.

In 1924 Isabella travelled to Montego Bay in Jamaica on an expedition to study sea urchins. This was quite an undertaking and a copy of her notes can be found in the archives of Keith Grammar School. In 1927-1928 she was a Research Fellow at Yale University working at the Woods Hole Oceanographic Centre and also at Stanford University in California. In 1928 she was awarded a DSc from Aberdeen University for 'The Development of the Skeleton in Echinoderms'.

Dr Gordon was a Principal Scientific Officer in charge of Crustacea in the Department of Zoology at the British Museum and was awarded an OBE in 1961 - a well deserved award.

In 1961 the Japanese Emperor Hirohito, himself a renowned marine biologist, celebrated his 60th birthday, and Dr Isabella Gordon of the British Museum of Natural History was invited to Japan for a face-to-face talk with the Emperor. This led to the establishment of the Carcinological Society of Japan for the purpose of promoting the study of the biology of crustaceans and fostering international relations. The Japanese were going to award her the Order of the Rising Sun but the UK Government blocked the honour.

Dr Isabella Gordon retired in 1966 and died in Carlisle in 1988. It was reported that she was known as 'The Grand Old Lady of Carcinology'.

Sea Urchin

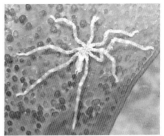

Sea Spider

Dr Isabella Gordon

Balloch Road where Isabella was born and brought up

PARSON JAMES GORDON
1617 – 1686

James Gordon was born 17th May 1617 at Kinmundy, Aberdeenshire, the son of Sir Robert Gordon of Straloch and Pitlurg. He was educated at King's College, Aberdeen, and was Minister of Rothiemay Church 1641-1686 and known locally as Parson Gordon.

His first wife, Margaret, was the sister of the Laird of Rothiemay, and they had three daughters. His second wife was Katherine Gordon with whom he had four sons and a daughter.

He was an author, having written 'Memoirs of Scots Affairs (1637-1641 in three volumes)'. James Gordon was also a gifted cartographer and was responsible for drawing the first map of Scotland, for inclusion in an atlas being compiled by the famous Dutch cartographer, Willem Bleau. He later received 500 merks for his drawing of a map of Edinburgh, and his settlement for a map of Aberdeen amounted to 20 ounces of silver, a silk hat and 'ane silk gown for his bed fellow'!

During the 1650's, English soldiers of Cromwell's Commonwealth commandeered his Manse and vandalised his church. In addition they 'dallied with the village girls and gambled in the alehouse' and their 'scandalous carriadge' generally caused havoc in the surrounding district.

He died on 26th September 1686. His burial place is unknown and so there is no gravestone, but his memory lives on in his writing and map-making.

A Cromwellian flag

**Scottish Coin
early 17th Century**

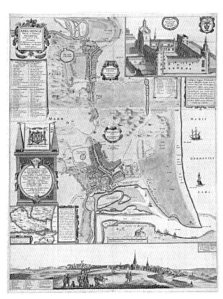

J. Gordon's map of Aberdeen 1661

J. Gordon's map of Edinburgh

Doorway and font from Rev. Gordon's church now located at the current Rothiemay church

REV. DR J.F.S. GORDON
1821 – 1904

James Frederick Skinner Gordon was born in Keith, son of John Gordon, Merchant and his wife Helen Skinner in 1821. His family was descended from the Gordons of Glenbucket. He received his basic education in the Keith Schools and progressed to Madras College in St Andrews. When only 15 years of age he gained the Grant Bursary at St Andrews University and graduated in 1840 with distinction. After further studies he gained MA in 1841 at St Andrews University. He was immediately appointed Organising Master of the Episcopal National School, Edinburgh, and, in 1843, was ordained a Deacon of the Scottish Episcopal Church and took up the position of Curate at Forres, Elginshire.

In 1844 he was elected incumbent at St Andrew's Episcopal Church, Glasgow, a position he retained until his retirement in 1890. In 1846, at Keith, he married Elspet Murdoch , daughter of the Rev. John Murdoch of Keith and Ruthven. He secondly married Miss Connolly, daughter of the Burgh Clerk of Anstruther.

St John's Episcopal Church, Forres

Rev. Gordon saw that industrialisation had brought large numbers of Anglican English and Irish followers to Glasgow, therefore he channelled his energies towards expanding the Scottish Episcopal Church. For the baptism of un-churched Episcopalians he was prepared to use slightly unorthodox methods at times. He was a pioneer in agitating for the demolition of slum buildings in Glasgow, which culminated in the introduction of the Glasgow Improvement Act, 1866.

In 1857, he received international Episcopalian recognition when the degree of Doctor of Divinity was conferred upon him by Hobart College, USA.

Rev. Gordon was a prolific writer. One of his works has great relevance to Keith and surrounding Parishes, usually known as 'The Chronicles of Keith', published in 1880. For this work the people of Keith and Parishes are extremely grateful, because of the information and history it contains. He was an ardent Freemason, having, as a student, been initiated in 1841 at St Andrews, and in this book there is a chapter devoted to this subject.

He also edited and extended, in 1882, a new edition of Lachlan Shaw's, 'History of the Province of Moray'.

He will always be remembered and admired for his philanthropic work in tending to the needs of the destitute, and for his literary career culminating in the publication of numerous books.

On his retirement in 1890, Rev. Gordon went to live in Beith, Ayrshire where he died on 23rd January 1904 and was interred with full Masonic Honours in Beith cemetery. He was possibly the oldest member of the Masons craft in the world.

Thus ended the life of a good man, born, educated and nurtured in Keith, Banffshire, who did so much to help his fellow man, and left a written legacy for the people of Keith and Parishes with the publication of 'The Book of the Chronicles of Keith, Grange, Ruthven, Cairney and Botriphnie'.

Holy Trinity, Keith

St Andrew's Episcopal Church, Glasgow

THE BOOK OF THE CHRONICLES

OF

K E I T H,

GRANGE, RUTHVEN, CAIRNEY,

AND

BOTRIPHNIE:

EVENTS, PLACES, AND PERSONS.

BY THE REV. J. F. S. GORDON, D.D.,
S. ANDREW'S, GLASGOW,
Author of Scotichronicon, Monasticon, Glasgow Facies, Monasticy, Sermons,
Pastorals, Letters, etc., etc.

GLASGOW:
ROBERT FORRESTER, 1 ROYAL EXCHANGE SQUARE.
1880.

57

LEWIS MORRISON GRANT
1872 – 1893

Lewis Morrison Grant was born at Loch Park Cottage, Botriphnie, on 9th December 1872 son of Lewis Grant and his wife Isabella Morrison.

In his tragically short life he proved to be a brilliant scholar and a fine poet. He was a very delicate young man, and his poetry sometimes reflected his sensitive nature and, some would say, his premonition of an early death.

When he was nine years old, he suffered a severe attack of pleurisy and nearly died. Five years later, having moved to Mill of Towie, he left Auchanacie School to attend Keith Public School. At sixteen he became ill again, preventing him from trying the university entry examination. However, he passed it in his eighteenth year and attended college at Aberdeen for two sessions.

In his second session in 1892 'Protomantis' was published and, returning home to Goldenwell, illness struck again, resulting in his death at the early age of twenty-one years. He is buried at Botriphnie.

His writings included 'A Dewdrop on a Rose'. A book titled 'Lewis Morrison Grant, his Life, Letters and Last Poems, 1894' was written by his friend, Miss Jessie Anne Anderson of Aberdeen. Such was his gift as a poet he was described as "Keats of the North".

**Loch Park Cottage
Botriphnie**

**Train approaching
Loch Park Cottage**

Lewis Morrison Grant

A DEWDROP ON A ROSE.

(Dedicated to James Kinlay, Kirkcaldy.)

A calm came o'er my spirit as I dreamed
  Within a city of the flowers whose bright
Streets, with the flush of even gilded, seemed
  All gold like heaven's. Meanwhile the mel
  Faded, and earth in the sun's fringes dight
Was, as she whilom was, a Paradise;
  She breathed so sweet, so gentle, like the flight
Of angels' wings—'twas hard to realize
That earth was one rent heart, and every breeze her sighs !

Goldenwell near Auchindachy

59

ROBERT GREEN
c 1797 – 1860

Robert Green was born in Aberlour c1797, to parents William Green and Helen (nee Stewart). He started a legal practice in Keith which became one of the most successful businesses in the County. He was appointed agent for the Union Bank in Keith. As well as being treasurer of the Parish Church, he was Factor for Mr Steuart of Auchlunkart and Major Gordon-Duff of Drummuir.

He was instrumental in financing the building of a female infant school located where Moss Street meets Church Road. Sadly Mr Green died in October 1860, five years before the school was completed. A public fund, generously subscribed to by the people of Keith and area, allowed the Robert Green project to be completed and the school was officially opened in 1865.

In 1924, the school was completely remodeled and opened as a Junior Primary School, and was known locally as, 'The Green School'.

Robert's wife was Elizabeth (nee Milne) and their only child, also Robert, died at the age of 26 in Lisbon.

With the official opening of the new Keith Primary School on 1st February 2012, the days of the old Green School as an educational establishment had drawn to a close. Although the future of this once handsome building is in doubt, Robert Green's vision for the education of young people remains just as relevant today.

**Junior Primary Department, Keith Grammar School
(The Green School)**

Union Bank and House with decorative mask

Date Stone Green School

Union Bank £1 note

Green School pupils 1890's

WALTER GREGOR
1825 – 1897

Walter Gregor was born on 23rd October 1825, the son of James Gregor, tenant farmer of Forgieside, Keith, and his wife Janet (nee Leslie). He attended Keith Public School and in 1845 he received a bursary to study at King's College, Aberdeen, where he graduated four years later with MA Honours. He was appointed as Master to Macduff School, a position he held for ten years. During this time he studied for the Ministry, and was ordained to Macduff Church in 1859, and moved to Pitsligo four years later.

The Rev. Gregor was an eminent scholar as well as a minister. The Natural Museum, Marischal College, Aberdeen was grateful to him for many valuable contributions, as he was an internationally-known natural historian, folklorist and archaeologist. He had an extensive knowledge of Scottish history, language, balladry and literature, especially that of his native Banffshire.

He had many books and pamphlets published in both English and French. Among his publications were, 'Dialect of Banffshire with a Glossary of Words not in Jamieson's Scottish Dictionary', 'Echo of Olden Times from the North of Scotland' and 'Notes on the Folklore of the North East of Scotland', to name but a few.

He was married to Margaret (nee Gardiner) and they had a son, Alexander, and a daughter, Janet. He retired to Bonnyrigg, Midlothian, and died there in 1897.

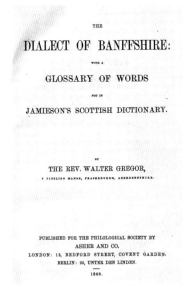

THE

DIALECT OF BANFFSHIRE:

WITH A

GLOSSARY OF WORDS

NOT IN

JAMIESON'S SCOTTISH DICTIONARY.

BY

THE REV. WALTER GREGOR,

F PITSLIGO MANSE, FRASERBURGH, ABERDEENSHIRE.

PUBLISHED FOR THE PHILOLOGICAL SOCIETY BY
ASHER AND CO.
LONDON: 13, BEDFORD STREET, COVENT GARDEN.
BERLIN: 20, UNTER DEN LINDEN.

1866.

Forgieside near Aultmore

Rothiemay children

Smachirie, *n.* a great number, particularly of what is of small size; as, "Sic a *smachirie* o' bairns is at the squeel." (Additional to Jamieson).

GILBERT HARROWER
1918 - 2007
Contributed by the late Alan Anderson

Gilbert Sowden Harrower was a Keith loon who left school at an early age and worked for a time in a grocer's shop.

The outbreak of war in 1939 saw him in The Gordon Highlanders, where he served with distinction as a signals sergeant. He was twice Mentioned in Dispatches and was particularly proud of one citation signed by Gen. Montgomery, Commander of the 8th Army in North Africa.

After the war he went to work at the Islabank Mills of G. & G. Kynoch Ltd. He attended the Scottish Woollen Technical College in Galashiels and graduated in the late 1940s. (The SWTC is now part of the Faculty of Textiles of the Heriot-Watt University and other ex-servicemen who studied there post war included W.L. Pawlowski, later managing director of Robert Laidlaw & Sons, and J.H. MacLennan, dyehouse manager at Laidlaws.)

On completion of his studies at Galashiels, Gilbert was appointed assistant manager at Kynochs, and much later became manager when John Scott retired.

In the early 1950s evening classes were started in Keith, to teach textile technology. The instructor was Gilbert and, over a number of years, he taught raw materials, yarn manufacture, weaving, designing, and finishing. Students included trainee warpers, drawers, loom tuners and designers. His classes were well attended in the early stages of the City and Guilds syllabus, but in the more advanced stages, numbers fell away as more time and commitment was needed. However, two of his students did go on to sit the final City & Guilds Design exams in 1958 and both passed, qualifying as designers. The SWTC that year published their names in their college awards list, although they had never attended the place!

In the more advanced stages of their studies, in addition to evening classes, Gilbert took those two students to his house at least once a week for extra tuition and his wife, Hilda, was generous with her cups of tea and biscuits.

In 1959 both students were awarded Full Technological Certificates of the City and Guilds Of London Institute. At the time, it was thought that they were the only two in Scotland ever to gain this award in textiles without attending college and Gilbert was justifiably proud of his work. He was subsequently offered an appointment as a lecturer in his old college at Galashiels, but chose to remain in Keith.

Before the war, Gilbert had been an assistant scoutmaster, and in the 1950s and 60s he helped with the running of the Boy Scouts in Keith. His main leisure activity was caravanning and he and his wife, Hilda, liked to spend weekends away. After his retirement they were able to spend longer periods enjoying stays in different areas.

Over a period of nearly ten years Gilbert taught several subjects, but not dyeing. This gap was filled when, in 1961, J. Henry MacLennan agreed to teach the subject. Like Gilbert he had served during the war but in the R.A.F., where he had been forced to bale out more than once, on one occasion landing in Japanese-occupied territory, but escaping capture. Those who sat the dyeing exam were again successful, including Gilbert's proteges.

The two men Gilbert trained did not let him down. One, Harry Thomson, stayed at Kynochs and became head designer when Robert (Bob) Weir retired in 1965. Harry was an active man with many interests. He liked golf, hill walking, climbing and ski-ing, played the bagpipes and enjoyed a game of chess. He died in 1994 aged 62 years leaving a widow and daughter.

Gilbert's other pupil decided to go into management and went on to study at the Aberdeen School of Management (part of the Robert Gordon University), where he gained a Post Graduate Diploma in Management Studies. He became a chartered Textile Technologist, an Associate of the Textile Institute and a Fellow of The Chartered Management Institute. He went on to hold numerous directorships, and served on several national and international committees related to wool textiles. Two other men in the Keith woollen mills were qualified C Text, ATI (Chartered Textile Technologist, Associate of the Textile Institute) — W.L. Pawlowski, and J.M. Kynoch.

Gilbert made a difference to the wool industry in his job as a manager of the biggest mill in Keith, but the work he did in textile education was also greatly appreciated, especially by his students, whose lives would have been different without his input. He died in September 2007, at the age of 89 years. A Gordons badge is engraved on his headstone which also bears the words 'A Stalwart Gordon Highlander'. He was proud of his regiment, as were many Keith men.

Gilbert was a staunch member of the Kirk of Keith, St Rufus, and there, in his capacity as an Elder, was respected and gave valued service to the church.

Gilbert at a Gordon Highlander event in Huntly

Gilbert and G.B. Kynoch

By the KING'S Order the name of
Corporal G. S. Harrower,
The Gordon Highlanders,
was published in the London Gazette on
13 January, 1944,
as mentioned in a Despatch for distinguished service.
I am charged to record
His Majesty's high appreciation.

Secretary of State for War

21st Army Group

2884115 Sjt. G. S. Harrower

5/7 Gordons

*It has been brought to my notice that you have
performed outstanding good service, and shown
great devotion to duty, during the campaign in
North West Europe.
I award you this certificate as a token of my
appreciation, and I have given instructions that
this shall be noted in your Record of Service.*

B. L. Montgomery

ALEXANDER HUMPHREY
1837 – 1902

Alexander Humphrey was born at Towiemore, Botriphnie, on 15th May 1837. He was educated at Botriphnie School and started his working life as an apprentice carpenter at Forkins, Botriphnie.

At the age of 25 he emigrated to New Zealand, where he invested in land and became wealthy.

In 1900 he returned to Scotland and married Jeannie Robb, daughter of James Robb, draper, at St James Masonic Lodge, Keith. They returned to New Zealand but sadly she died in Wellington just over a year later. Alexander passed away in Napier, New Zealand shortly afterwards on the 24th October 1902.

He never forgot his native land and, on his death he bequeathed a sum of £2,000 to Botriphnie Parish, to be used as scholarships and to finance the building of a gymnasium or swimming pool. A portrait hangs in the gymnasium (now a classroom) in Botriphnie School.

Towiemore Farm

68

Forkins

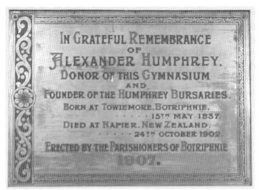

IN GRATEFUL REMEMBRANCE
OF
ALEXANDER HUMPHREY.
DONOR OF THIS GYMNASIUM
AND
FOUNDER OF THE HUMPHREY BURSARIES.
BORN AT TOWIEMORE, BOTRIPHNIE,
· · · · · 15TH MAY 1837.
DIED AT NAPIER, NEW ZEALAND,
· · · · · 24TH OCTOBER 1902.
ERECTED BY THE PARISHIONERS OF BOTRIPHNIE
1907.

Plaque inside Botriphnie School gymnasium

School gymnasium

ALICE HUNTER
1883 – 1972

Alice Hunter was born at Botriphnie Schoolhouse on 19th March 1883, daughter of John Robertson Hunter and his wife, Ann Farquharson. It was in this parish that Alice would spend her childhood years and receive her education. Her father, John, was the highly esteemed headmaster of Botriphnie School, Inspector of the Poor, Registrar and also ran evening classes in his school. He had a deep admiration for, and an abiding interest in, the people of the parish. Despite the hardships which the families endured, they exhibited great fortitude and always kept the education of their children to the forefront of their ambitions. When Alice, the youngest of the family, was 12 years old, her father died of typhoid. He was only 42 years old and was buried in the graveyard of his beloved Botriphnie.

After her father's death, it is thought that Alice and her family moved to Aberdeen, where the family had roots, because, in 1903, it was recorded that her mother, aged 53 years, died at a house in Aberdeen. Alice continued her education and became an elementary school teacher. She married William C. Forbes, a lawyer, on 27th December 1912. Little is known of their life together, although it would seem that there were no children.

Alice Hunter Forbes was the only member of the Hunter family to reach old age and when she died in 1972 she left a substantial legacy for the benefit of the poor in Botriphnie parish. Perhaps Alice was mindful of her father's concern for the hardship endured by the less well off people of Botriphnie and tried to ease that load with her bequest.

The 'Hunter Bequest' is processed, and distributed annually, by Botriphnie Parish Church and today provides a 'Christmas Box' for the elderly of the parish.

Botriphnie School Board and date plaques

Botriphnie School

The Dominie and his family outside Botriphnie Schoolhouse

JOSEPH "SHOTTIE" HUNTER
1847 – 1923

Joseph Hunter was born in Bagraw, Northumberland on 11th November 1847. When he became an adult, he began work in the local mills. Keen to better his situation, in 1871 he came north, to Keith in Scotland, and found employment at Kynochs, Isla Bank Mill. He was a reliable worker and soon was promoted to warping foreman.

In 1881 he married Annie Grant Walker and, soon afterwards, decided to branch out on his own. He bought the Old Town Mill, also known as the Glebe Mill, on the banks of the River Isla near the Old Kirk of Keith and close to what is now Strathmill Distillery. It became a great success. Joseph Hunter was well liked in the town and his mill was affectionately known as 'Shottie Hunter's Mill'.The nickname came about as follows: the thickness and texture of the cloth was dependent on the type of wool used and the number of strands per inch. Joseph was able to achieve up to 36 'shots' (strands) per inch of material, hence the nickname "Shottie".

During a storm in 1910, the River Isla flooded the wool mill, ruining the merchandise and the machinery. It was at this point that Joseph Hunter decided to give up the business, and he closed the Mill and set about trading in woollen goods, with considerable success.

The mill fell into ruin, but the path of the lade (water channel) can still be seen on the banks of the River Isla.

Joseph Hunter died on 11th June 1923 in Turner Memorial Hospital and was buried in Broomhill cemetery.

**Weaving Industry
Commemorative stone in Reidhaven Square**

Glebe Mill

GEORGE JAMIESON
1843 – 1920

George Jamieson was born in 1843, son of Alexander Jamieson farmer, Crannoch, Grange and his wife, Helen Pirie. George was educated at Grange Parish School. In 1864, he graduated from Aberdeen University with an honours degree in mathematics, having been awarded The Boxhill Prize of £35. That year he travelled to China to take up a position in the Consular Service. He returned to Britain in 1871 and trained as a barrister in London. In 1873 he married Margaret Inkson of Berryleys, Grange. In late 1873 he returned to Shanghai and in 1879 became Vice-Consul in Foochow. Two years later he became Consul at Kiukiang. He was so well respected by the local merchants that they presented him with an Address and a symbolic Red Umbrella, in appreciation of his commitment to their cause.

After a further ten years, in 1891, he was appointed Assistant Judge at the British Supreme Court for China and Japan, and H.M. Consul, Shanghai. He was the author of a treatise, 'The Silver Question', for which, in 1895, he was awarded a £50 prize offered by Sir Henry Meysey-Thomson.

In 1897, he became the Head of H.M. Consular Services in Shanghai and, that same year, in honour of her Diamond Jubilee, Queen Victoria made Mr George Jamieson, a 'Companion of the Order of St Michael and St George'.

Highly respected by Westminster, in 1898 he was appointed Commercial Attache to China.

He retired to London, having spent thirty-four years in the Far East. During that time he never forgot his roots and gave generously to his former school. He died in December 1920.

His grandson was Hugh Gaitskell, Leader of the Labour Party from 1955 to 1963.

Flag of China

British Consulate in Shanghai

**Order of
St Michael & St George**

DAVID M. KING
c1857 – 1929

David Mackenzie King was born son of James King and his wife Mary Russell, at Garrowood, Grange, about 1857. He was educated at a dame school and later tutored by a Mr David Gerrard. Mr King was employed in the offices of Mr Paull, Advocate, Aberdeen, and advanced to take over management of one of Mr Paull's interests, namely, a laundry business. He moved to England and made his fortune, but never forgot the folk of Grange.

He financed the site, erection and upkeep of the King Memorial Hall, which was completed in 1925 and opened by His Grace, The Duke of Richmond and Gordon, for the use of the people of Grange, Rothiemay and Cairnie.

Mr. King was held in high esteem by his employees who presented him with the engraved plaque which is now displayed in the foyer of the hall. Brass plaques are also displayed in the hall, commemorating the fallen of the three parishes in the two World Wars.

A highly respected employer, and generous benefactor, he died in London on 9th May 1929, and his ashes were buried in Rothiemay Churchyard.

David King

King Memorial Hall

THE KYNOCH FAMILY IN KEITH

1786 George Kynoch was born at Tanfield, near Aberdeen, the son of John Kynoch, a farmer, and his wife, Agnes Milne.

1788 Morrison, Mason & Co established a Bleachfield on the banks of the River Isla at Keith to process linen manufactured in North East Scotland.

1805 George came to Keith and set up in business as a tin and coppersmith. For a time he was the tenant of the farm of Little Forgie, but his main business became that of grocer and provision merchant in Mid Street (George Kynoch & Son). Later he had shares in the distillery, now known as Strathmill, and also developed a sea trade with England in grain and coal.

**George Kynoch
1786 - 1859**

1807 George married Elspet Keith, originally from Grange.

1810 They had seven children including George, born in 1810, and Robert Keith Kynoch, who became a doctor of medicine. Another son, Alexander, inherited his father's merchant business in Mid Street, and later became the proprietor of Greenton, now known as Greenwood, just outside Keith. Alexander's wife was Magdalene Stephen and one of their daughters, Agnes, married Dr Robert Turner, after whom the local hospital was named.

1811 George Kynoch, coppersmith, was admitted to membership of The Domestic Friendly Society of Keith.

1826 The Bleachfield passed from the original company, through a Mr Esson, to George Kelman, who had a small business in bleaching, wool carding and cloth manufacturing.

1833 George Kynoch Jnr married Anne Milne, a native of Peterhead. At first he was also a tin and coppersmith, but later ran an extensive business dealing in leather, at 92 Mid Street.

1836 George Jnr and Anne's son, George Nicol Kynoch, was born.

1840 A second son, Robert, was born. When very young, Robert inherited Hillside of Portlethen in Kincardineshire and adopted the surname Kynoch Shand.

1849 George Jnr established a fertiliser business at the Tannachy Bone Mill at Portgordon, using imported guano and bonemeal. This business was managed, along with a Mr Alexander Christie, until the latter retired in 1853, although the partnership was not dissolved until 1858.

Islabank Manure Works

1858 A new partnership with his son, George Nicol Kynoch, was set up as G & G Kynoch. The lease of the Keith Bleachfield, and the adjacent carding wool mill, came on the market, and was considered to be a suitable central storage site for the Kynochs' Banffshire operations. George Kelman, the previous tenant, insisted the mill be taken over as a working concern. This took place at Martinmas 1858. There are still two stones, set into the wall of the old mill, recording this event.

1859 George Kynoch Snr died at his home in Land Street, Keith, aged 73.

1862 The trade at the Carding Wool Mill had prospered so much that the mill was refurbished and expanded to include cloth making. It was renamed Isla Bank Mills. By this time, they had sold their leather business at 92 Mid Street.

Datestone

1867 Alexander Kynoch died aged 52. His widow, Magdalene, carried on the business of George Kynoch & Son until 1874. Their eldest daughter, Mary, married Thomas Abercrombie Petrie Hay of Edintore. He took over the running of the business, and later became the first Provost of Keith in 1889.

1873 The Longmore Hall was completed at a cost of £2,000 and presented to the town by William Longmore. The first Chairman of the Trustees of the Hall was George Kynoch.

1874 George Kynoch retired (he died in 1883) and the Mills were now run by George Nicol Kynoch and his brother, Robert Kynoch Shand.

1875 George Nicol Kynoch married Edith Wheen. Workers' cottages, erected near the Mill, were named Edithfield Cottages.

1878 Robert Kynoch Shand built Linn House. George and Edith's son, John Wheen Kynoch, was born.

1883 Philip Kynoch Shand was born, son of Robert Kynoch Shand

**George Kynoch
1810 - 1883**

1886 The Keith Institute was opened. George Nicol Kynoch was an original director of the Keith Institute Company.

1888 George became a director of the Highland Railway.

1890 Robert Kynoch Shand died very suddenly aged 49, leaving George alone at the helm.

1893 George Nicol Kynoch funded the erection of two fever wards at Turner Memorial Hospital (built in 1880) as "an expression of gratitude to Almighty God for his escape from the recent railway accident at Thirsk". They were named, 'The Kynoch Wards'. He died later that year in London. The Mills were now being run by Trustees until cousins, John Wheen Kynoch and Philip Kynoch Shand, were old enough to take charge. Later John went on to study at the

Yorkshire Textile College in Leeds and also at a textile establishment in Germany.

1900 The wage around this time, for a female mill worker, was between 14/- and 16/- per week, according to experience and ability.

1900 John Kynoch married Mary Percival Marriott and they had three children, Gladys, Gordon and Oswald. Gladys married the Minister of St Rufus Church, Rev. Matthew Stewart, who later became Moderator of the General Assembly of the Church of Scotland. In 1958 she had the Matthew Stewart Memorial Gardens laid out in memory of her late husband, and gifted Church Cottage, now the St Rufus Manse, to the Kirk. Oswald emigrated to New Zealand and became a sheep farmer.

Mary P. Kynoch

1909 Cousins, John and Philip, were joined on the Board by Charles E. Winter, as head of sales, based in London.

1914-1918 During World War I the Mill had full employment and was extremely busy, weaving material and blankets for servicemen, and collecting sphagnum moss for use in the dressing of battle-wounds.

1925 G & G Kynoch became a private limited company. Charles Winter's sons, Edgar and Geoffrey, were appointed to the Board.

1929 John Kynoch's son, Gordon Bryson Kynoch, was appointed an ordinary director.

1931 The Kynoch Scottie Dog trademark / logo was introduced.

1931 The Depression saw a serious shortage of work, and many employees were working on a day–to–day basis.

1933   Oswald's son, John Marriott Kynoch, was born in New Zealand.

1939 John W. Kynoch received a Knighthood for political and public service in North East Scotland. Philip Kynoch Shand died, and Gordon Kynoch took over responsibility for the Mills.

1939-1945 During World War II, Isla Bank Mills were very busy manufacturing and producing khaki cloth. Air raid shelters were built, and black-out blinds covered windows and doorways. G. B. Kynoch served with the Gordon Highlanders in India and Burma, and returned as a Lieutenant Colonel, to command the Home Guard in Banffshire, until it was disbanded.

John W. Kynoch

1946 Sir John Kynoch died and was succeeded by his son Gordon.

1952 John Marriott Kynoch from New Zealand joined the company.

1954   G & G Kynoch became a public company.

1961 Lt. Col. Gordon Kynoch was made a CBE in the New Year Honours.

1966 The company received the Queen's Award for Industry for achievements in exports. It was the first woollen manufacturer in Scotland to achieve this distinction.

1960/70s These two decades were marked by a modernisation programme which saw the installation of several modern machines, including heat setting machinery, spinning frames and high speed shuttleless looms. These looms could insert weft three times as fast as the old Dobcross Looms, which had been in use for the previous hundred years. Later, during this period, there were many factors world wide which affected the industry. This caused a steady decline in the textile industry, both nationally and locally, and, along with galloping inflation, meant urgent changes were required.

1975 G. B. Kynoch, who had been Provost of Keith from 1967 to 1971, received the Freedom of the Town, along with Provost Ian Robertson, prior to the reorganisation of local government in May 1975.

1977 The board of directors was restructured. G. B. Kynoch became chairman of the company. His son George and his nephew John were appointed joint managing directors, along with William Winter.

1979 Another disappointing year, with many other textile companies going out of business.

1980 Gordon Hay succeeded G. B. Kynoch as Chairman, George was appointed Chief Executive, and a three-year recovery period was set in motion.

1986 With increased investment and better marketing, the future of the Mill began to improve.

1988 Two hundred years on from the establishment of the Keith Bleachfield, Chief Executive George

Gordon B. Kynoch

Kynoch, and Chairman, Gordon Hay, foresaw a brighter future. This was celebrated by the publishing of a history of the Isla Bank Mills, entitled, 'Two Hundred Years of Kynoch - A Scottish Textile Story'.

1991 Despite earlier optimism, manufacturing ceased. The plant and machinery were auctioned. A small design and sales team was retained in Keith, and renamed Kynoch Textiles. G & G Kynoch Ltd. was re-branded as Kynoch Group and moved to Andover in Kent, where it produced health care products. In August Kynoch Textiles was bought by Joshua Ellis, a well-respected Yorkshire manufacturer, but closed shortly afterwards.

1992 George Kynoch became an MP and, in 1995, Minister of State at the Scottish Office with responsibility for industry. He later served as Vice Chairman of the Conservative Party in Scotland.

1998 Lt. Col. Gordon Bryson Kynoch died.

Over two hundred years of the textile industry on the banks of the River Isla in Keith was no more – truly the end of an era!

Islabank Mills, Edithfield and Keith Junction Station

Islabank House

Linn House

JOHN MARRIOTT KYNOCH
1933 -
Contributed by the late Alan Anderson

John Kynoch was born in 1933 and brought up in the Hawkes Bay area of the North Island of New Zealand. His father, Oswald, was the son of Sir John W. Kynoch of Isla Bank, and brother of Lt. Col. G.B. Kynoch. Oswald had emigrated to the Antipodes as a young man and farmed a large sheep station.

Before coming to Scotland to stay in the early 1950s, John studied wool at a college in New Zealand. When he came here to work at Isla Bank Mills, he spent time in each of the yarn production departments in order to gain practical experience. He also attended the Scottish Woollen Technical College in Galashiels (now part of the Faculty of Textiles of Heriot Watt University.) John later qualified as a Chartered Textile Technologist and became an Associate of the Textile Institute. In time he was appointed to the Board of G. & G. Kynoch and served as a director until 1982, when having been made redundant, he went to Basingstoke and set up a printing business.

He was an active man who enjoyed rugby, cricket, hill walking and shooting. At the Olympic Games in Munich, in 1972, he won a Bronze Medal for 50m Running Target rifle shooting. It was the first medal of those games to come to Britain, and was widely headlined, earning John well-deserved acclaim.

His wife, Jocelyn, also from New Zealand, was a prominent member of the WRVS in Keith, and in Moray. John took an active interest in local clubs and served as a town councillor in Keith, following the example of his uncle, Lt. Col. G.B. Kynoch, his grandfather, Sir John Kynoch, his grandmother, Mary P. Kynoch and his great-grandfather, George N. Kynoch.

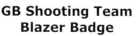

**GB Shooting Team
Blazer Badge**

**Munich Medal Ceremony 1972
John with gold medalist
Yakov Zheleznyak**

**John with Winans Cup
at Bisley in 2008**

Running Boar target shooting

THE LAIDLAW FAMILY

1828 Robert Laidlaw was born in the Vale of Yarrow, Selkirkshire and learned the art of handloom weaving from an uncle.

1845 He moved to a mill in Galashiels and worked there for 15 years.

1860 Robert went to work for James Daziel & Sons at Tweedholm Wool Mill in the small village of Walkerburn, near Peebles, and subsequently became manager of that mill.

1880 Robert moved north to take up an appointment with James Johnston & Co. in Elgin.

1882   He had always harboured a desire to have his own mill. The opportunity presented itself when the Mill and Croft at Bridge of Isla, Rothiemay became available to rent. Along with his wife Mary and family, Adam, Helen, Bessie and John, he took up the lease of the mill. It was in poor condition with old fashioned equipment. The water from the River Isla driving the mill could not always be relied upon as summer drought and winter frost limited the reliability of the power source. Modernisation of the plant and buildings was required but the owner James Sharpe, an ex-schoolmaster, would not agree to share the cost.

Laidlaws Mill, Bridge of Isla, Rothiemay

1890 Robert's elder son, Adam, leased the Fife Mills in Dufftown, where he manufactured fabrics from yarn spun at Rothiemay.

1900 The Rothiemay Mill had grown steadily, and Robert realised the need for expansion and modernisation of equipment. By the end of the year his mind was made up, and a site was secured on Seafield Estate ground in the nearby town of Keith and named Seafield Mills in honour of the Countess of Seafield.

Adam   **John**
Sons of the founder Robert Laidlaw

1901 January saw the new mill begin operations, and in June it was announced that the work of the Fife Mill, in Dufftown, was to be transferred to the Keith mill. The Rothiemay branch was retained.

1914 During the first years in Keith growth was slow, and just as business was picking up, World War I broke out. From then until 1918 normal trade diminished and the mill began to make army blankets. Output was small and machinery poor, so little profit was made.

1919 After the War ended, the buildings were extended and a new carding machine installed in the hope of expansion but the Depression dashed these hopes. Quite a lot of work during this period consisted of spinning and weaving for local farmers.

1930 Yarn spinning for trade customers became a major part of the mill's workload and the smaller local work was gradually phased out.

1933 The wider scope of business saw rapid progress, and large extensions to the preparation and dyehouse departments were built. There was no public electricity supply, so an A.C. generating plant was installed to supply current for the modern machinery.

1935 A programme of expansion and modernisation was initiated under the management of Adam's sons Roy A. Laidlaw and S. Graham Laidlaw. Warehouse and office blocks were built.

1938 The spinning and carding sheds were extended.

1939 Major expansion plans were put on hold as World War II was declared.

1945 Redevelopment plans began. New carding and spinning sheds with new machinery were built. Weaving was transferred to the old carding shed and the finishing plant moved to the old loom sheds. All the machinery was now driven by electricity and it was thought to be the first Scottish mill to use this form of power.

1950 Robert Laidlaw & Sons bought Scottish Crofter-Weavers where single-width Harris Tweed-type fabric was hand-woven in Lewis and Harris from yarn spun in Keith and then the cloth was brought back to Keith for finishing. In 1958 the Court of Session in Edinburgh ruled that Harris Tweed had to be produced wholly in the

Aeriel view of Seafield Mills and Keith 1949.

Outer Hebrides which led to the demise of this enterprise.

1952 Dyehouse built by B. Paterson, Newmill.

1960 The firm of Robert Laidlaw & Sons was sold to Grampian Holdings, a Glasgow based conglomerate. Graham Laidlaw retired and Roy Laidlaw remained as Managing Director for a year until he too retired.

1960s Continuing expansion during the decade with:

    1961 New Woolstore
    1962 New extension to the Weaving Department
    1963 New Wareroom
    1969 New Dyehouse

1970 During the next few years the company had several different owners but sadly success eluded them.

1978 Three directors bought Robert Laidlaw & Sons and at that time it employed 200 people and was a mainstay of the local economy.

1982 Robert Laidlaw & Sons celebrated their centenary, 100 years since taking over the mill at Bridge of Isla, Rothiemay.

1991 A decision to cease yarn manufacture was made by Clissold & Son. Grampian Regional Council purchased the building and leased part of it back to Robert Laidlaw & Sons. Clissolds sold the spinning business to two managers who ran it as Grampian Yarns.

1994 Clissolds retained the cloth manufacturing part of the business until 1994, when they sold it to two other managers. This ended Clissolds association with the site. The name Robert Laidlaw & Sons went to England. The new company was named Seafield of Scotland.

1995 Grampian Yarns traded in the U.K. and abroad, but suffered badly when their biggest customer went into receivership, owing them a large sum of money. In December 1995, Grampian Yarns ran out of funds and the business closed.

1998 The owners of both Grampian Yarns and Seafield of Scotland had worked very hard to keep the mills running to provide much needed employment in Keith, but enthusiasm and hard work were not enough.

1998 Seafield of Scotland ran out of funds and business ceased.

2008 On the site of the prestigious mill there now stands a Tesco supermarket store. They have thoughtfully preserved, and inserted into two ornamental walls at the entrance, the six date stones denoting the expansion phases of the Robert Laidlaw & Sons, Seafield Mills.

ROBERT LAIDLAW, *Woollen Manufacturer,*
BRIDGE OF ISLA MILLS, ROTHIEMAY.

Woolstore

Weft Winding

Finishing

Weaving

LORD IRVINE LAIDLAW
1943 –

Irvine Alan Stewart Laidlaw was born in Keith in 1943, the son of Robert (Roy) Alan Laidlaw and grandson of Adam Laidlaw. He was the great-grandson of Robert Laidlaw, who had leased the Wool Mill at Rothiemay in 1882 before moving to Keith in 1901 to set up Seafield Mills.

After a private education at Merchiston Castle School, Edinburgh, he gained a BA at the University of Leeds. Irvine Laidlaw then chose not to join the family business. Instead he set off to carve a career for himself in the USA, where he embarked on a post-graduate course at Columbia University. After some time exploring other employment opportunities, in 1973 he purchased a small newsletter business, which he turned into 'The Institute for International Research'. This business expanded into the

Baron Laidlaw of Rothiemay

world's largest conference organiser, a global leader in skills and knowledge transfer, making Irvine Laidlaw a multi-millionaire. He disposed of the businesses in 2005.

In 2004 he was made a life peer, as Baron Laidlaw of Rothiemay. Lord Irvine Laidlaw has become a leading Scottish philanthropist and set up the Laidlaw Youth Project. Keith was not forgotten by this benefactor, as he provided a five figure sum to set up the Loft Project in Mid Street, to help employ a support worker specialising in befriending and mentoring users of the drop-in centre for young people. This project took over the Craighurst Restaurant in Mid Street, and trained young people in all aspects of work in the catering industry.

Lord Laidlaw was aware of the problems facing Keith, with the loss of the Isla Bank and Seafield Mills, both mainstays of the town economy. In 2005 he gave £40,000 which, along with other sources, including the European Social Fund, helped to create the Isla Bank Skills Centre in Keith, under the banner of Banff & Buchan College. This venture was set up to teach young people vocational and practical skills, thus enabling them to find employment. In September 2006, Lord Laidlaw re-visited his home town and officially opened the Isla Bank Skills Centre.

In July 2007, Aberdeen University bestowed on Lord Irvine Laidlaw an honorary doctorate for his philanthropic work. In 2010 he stepped down from the House of Lords but retained his title.

Lord Laidlaw in Mid Street 2006
(Courtesy of Banffshire Herald)

WILLIAM LONGMORE
1806 – 1882

William Longmore was born on 13th November 1806 at Burnside, Enzie, the son of William and Mary (nee Chalmers). His paternal grandparents, William and Margaret Longmore, farmed at Brae, Keith. The tenancy eventually passed to grandson William, but he decided that farming wasn't for him and instead took up employment with Mr J.W. Cowie, Solicitor.

He later emigrated to New Orleans, but ill health forced him to return to his native Banffshire, where he became a businessman and benefactor.

In 1835, he became Agent for the North of Scotland Bank and held this post until his death. He was Chairman of the Keith Gas Company and a director of the Great North of Scotland Railway Company. He acquired Milton Distillery (now known as Strathisla Distillery) and was responsible for building improvements and introducing new machinery.

His deep interest in the welfare of the people of Keith made him a popular and highly respected gentleman, and he was a very generous benefactor, gifting the Longmore Hall in 1873 and six years later, the Keith Bowling Green.

Mr Longmore was instrumental in the forming of a committee for the proposed building of Turner Memorial Hospital and gave generously to the building fund. On completion of the hospital building he was the first President of its Board of Directors. He was also Hon. Sheriff Substitute and a Justice of the Peace.

He was married firstly, to Helen Lemmon and they had one daughter, Anne, and two sons, Adam and William. Helen died in 1848 and, in 1860, he married Jane Munro, daughter of a Huntly minister, and they had one daughter, Jane. William Longmore died in Keith on 23rd December 1882 and was buried in the Old Keith Cemetery, 'a quiet and unassuming gentleman'.

Bowling Green

**North of Scotland Bank
Moss Street**

William Longmore

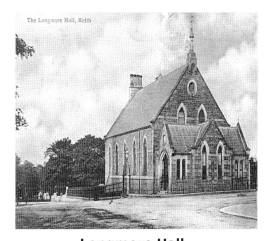

Longmore Hall

Milton Distillery

JANET McKAY
1886 - 1936

Jessie Munro McKay was born on 8th June 1886 in Land Street, Keith, the daughter of George McKay and his wife, Jessie Munro.

George was a very successful master plasterer, becoming an elder of the Free Church and serving as a Keith town councillor from 1902 till his death in 1909. The McKay family, in which there were eleven children in total, lived at Moorfield in Land Street, which they rebuilt in 1895.

Young Jessie (or Janet as she was later known) was educated at Keith Grammar School. Aged 24 and following in the footsteps of others at this time, she travelled across the Atlantic to America to become a lady's companion.

In World War I Janet enrolled as a nurse and was three times mentioned by the American Red Cross and the French Government for 'conspicuous services'.

When the Armistice with the Ottoman Empire came into effect in 1918, Janet Mckay was one of the first people to be sent by American Near East Relief to Alexandropol in newly-independent Armenia to organise emergency aid. Between 1915 and 1930 Near East Relief administered $117 million of assistance throughout the region with food, clothing, shelters, relief camps, medical aid, hospitals and clinics, as well as orphanages and vocational training. When Janet arrived in Alexandropol she was confronted by a dire humanitarian crisis: 200,000 starving refugees, of whom 25,000 were hospital cases, in a city with not a single nurse, doctor, hospital or any medical supplies. The refugee population was riddled with diseases ranging from cholera and malaria to smallpox, tuberculosis and typhus.

Moorfield, Land Street

With characteristic determination and organizational ability, Janet, along with one American doctor, commandeered an abandoned and derelict hospital building. With the help of refugee labour, this was quickly transformed into a working medical facility. Janet was head nurse in the section treating the eye condition, trachoma, which affected almost three quarters of the orphanage population.

Near East Relief then addressed the orphan situation and took over the three former Russian army barracks in the city - Polygon, Kazachiy Post and Severskiy - and soon an orphanage city housing 22,000 was established. It was probably the largest orphanage in the world.

The convoluted political situation did not help. The Turkish-Armenian War of 1920 resulted in 200,000 deaths and Turkish military occupation. After the Treaty of Kars in 1921 Alexandropol was taken over by the Armenian Soviet Socialist Republic. The Armenian SSR merged with Georgia and Azerbaijan to become the Transcaucasian Socialist Federative Soviet Republic, (TSFSR), which in 1922 was one of the four founding republics of the Soviet Union. Through all this turmoil and uncertainty Janet and Near East Relief continued to care for their orphan charges. In 1924

TSFSR Flag

99

Alexandropol was renamed Leninakan in honour of the recently-deceased Soviet leader, Vladimir Lenin.

Alexandropol

In 1925 Near East Relief began to release children back into the community, placing them with Armenian families either for adoption or fostering or into work situations. As director of the Child Welfare Department, she also arranged for their continuing medical care by organising a travelling clinic.

On 22nd October 1926 an earthquake struck the region. The shocks lasted several hours with twelve towns completely destroyed, thirteen others partially destroyed, 350 people killed, 400 injured and 100,000 made homeless. During the devastation Janet McKay, "with great courage and determination", escorted her young children from the orphanage buildings out into safety and led them in singing Armenian folk-songs to keep up their spirits amid the aftershocks.

Her ability to communicate and relate to her children resulted in the almost total elimination of the institutional element of the Leninakan orphanages, so much so, that she was known as 'The Mother of Six Thousand Children'.

When she left the city to return home to New Haven, Connecticut, in November 1929, a farewell dinner was attended by all the departments of the local authority who

Children waiting in the snow for admission into Orphan City

named a street in her honour, such was the esteem in which she was held. It was reported that, when they heard that their 'Mother' was leaving them after ten years, twelve thousand children wept for three days.

Janet McKay became Principal of the Tudor City Children's Clinic in New York. Tragically she died in a road accident on 27th July 1936. Janet never married, preferring 'to make many happy instead of one'.

Mealtime

Orphan City Playground

JAMES MACKINTOSH
1856 – 1924

James Mackintosh was born in Keith on 10th June 1856, and moved to Newmill at the age of 6 years. He was educated at Newmill and Keith schools, before starting his working life on local farms. He was employed at Auchoynanie and other neighbouring farms. In 1877, aged 21, he joined The Perthshire Constabulary.

In October 1881 he left Scotland for Cape Colony in southern Africa and joined the Cape Government Railway Service in Port Elizabeth. At that time the railway system was undergoing a period of rapid expansion as the government sought to create a network to link the diamond and gold fields in the interior to the Cape Colony ports.

James was largely responsible for the introduction of the Co-operative Movement. He was associated with the North End Library in Port Elizabeth from its inception, firstly as a member of the committee, then as chairman and later as Librarian.

Such was the esteem in which he was held, that a portrait of him was unveiled by the Mayor (a personal friend) in recognition of his life and service to the public. James Mackintosh died on 9th September 1924.

Port Elizabeth 1877

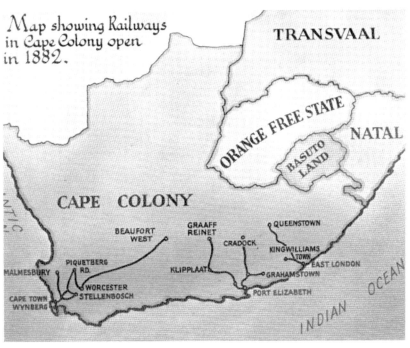

Map showing Railways
in Cape Colony open
in 1882.

TRANSVAAL

ORANGE FREE STATE

NATAL

BASUTO LAND

CAPE COLONY

BEAUFORT WEST

GRAAFF REINET

CRADOCK

QUEENSTOWN

KINGWILLIAMS TOWN

KLIPPLAAT

EAST LONDON

PIQUETBERG RD.

MALMESBURY

GRAHAMSTOWN

WORCESTER STELLENBOSCH

PORT ELIZABETH

CAPE TOWN WYNBERG

INDIAN OCEAN

JOHN MACKINTOSH
1833 – 1907

John Mackintosh was born in a thatched cottage in the Gateside area of the Parish of Botriphnie, on the 9th November 1833, son of William and Ann (nee Edward). His father had served for 14 years in the Army. He had been wounded three times in the Peninsular Campaign in Spain and Portugal. Shortly after the battle of Vittoria he retired on a small pension and and set up a school at Gateside. John was educated at Botriphnie Parish School and, aged 10 years, he became a cowherd. When he was 17 years old he was apprenticed as a shoemaker, a trade he continued for 14 years in various parts of the country.

With his interest in books and learning, he joined literary and debating societies, and moved to Aberdeen. In 1864 he enlisted in the City of Aberdeen Police Force. In 1869 he took over a stationery business in the Gallowgate, later transferring to Broad Street and finally to King Street. He was twice married, first to Elspet Bannerman and secondly, in 1885, to Grace Knight and they had two daughters.

His continued love of books and learning led to the publication of his own books, four volumes of, 'The History of Civilisation in Scotland'. This publication was used for a time as a text book by history students at the university. His knowledge was greatly respected by both students and professors. He also wrote other works and in 1888 the Senatus Academicus of Aberdeen University conferred on Mackintosh the honorary degree of Doctor of Laws.

In recognition of his contribution to the literary services, a portrait in oils, along with a considerable sum of money, was presented to him in June 1904. For some time this portrait had pride of place in the Central Library in Aberdeen.

Dr John Mackintosh died on 4 May 1907, aged 74 years.

Broad Street

Gallowgate

THE HISTORY

OF

CIVILISATION IN SCOTLAND.

BY

JOHN MACKINTOSH.

•

VOL. II.

ABERDEEN:
A. BROWN & CO.
1880.

[All Rights Reserved.]

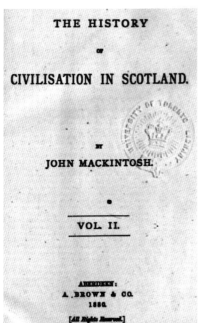

Aberdeen Central Library 1892
opened by Andrew Carnegie.

GEORGE MACLEAN
1801 - 1847
Contributed by Ron Smith

George MacLean was born in Keith on the 24th February 1801, the fifth of seven children of Rev. James MacLean, and his wife, Elizabeth (nee Tod) who came from Stankhouse, Birnie.

Rev. James MacLean had been given the charge of the Established Church of Keith in January 1795, and was the first minister of the new St Rufus Church, built in 1816 - 1819. He later moved to Urquhart Church.

George grew up and received his education in Keith, possibly from his father, from private tutors or at the Parish School situated at that time above the Tollbooth in Keith Square.

He joined the army on the 18th January 1815 and served in an Irish regiment during the Napoleonic wars, but saw no action. In 1826, he joined the Royal African Colonial Corps and was sent to Sierra Leone, and then the Gold Coast (now known as Ghana), where, after a short time, he was appointed Chief Administrator/Governor from 1830-1844. During this period he brought stability to the country and was involved in continuing the suppression of the slave trade. George became ill in 1838 and had to return to Britain for a time to convalesce.

He married Letitia Landon, a well-known authoress, on 7th June 1838 in London, and both returned to the Gold Coast. Sadly Letitia died there on 15th October 1838 of prussic acid poisoning. George died of dysentery in 1847 and was buried in Cape Coast Castle.

George MacLean was renowned for introducing the Judicial System and the Bond of 1844, which forms the basis of the modern Ghanaian Constitution.

A booklet on George MacLean has been written by Ron Smith of Keith & District Heritage Group.

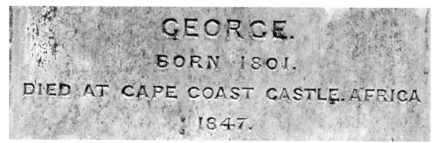

Detail from MacLean family memorial in Keith Old Cemetery

George MacLean

Letitia Landon

Keith Auld Kirk

Tolbooth in Keith Square

JOHN MACLEOD 1876 – 1935
Joint Nobel Prize Winner 1923

John James Rickard Macleod was born on the 6th September 1876, at Cluny, near Dunkeld in Perthshire, and was the eldest son of the Rev. Robert Macleod.

In October 1879, when he was just three years old, John and his family moved to Keith. His father had been called to the Free Church in Keith, to be their minister. This is now Keith North Church.

Here in the town of Keith, John would have received a brief introduction to his education, possibly at the Green Primary School, as the Free Church School on Union Street would have closed when the 1872 Education Act came into force.

When he was about seven years old, in 1883, the family moved once more, as his father had been called to another position in Aberdeen.

While at Aberdeen Grammar School, John proved to be an outstanding pupil and from there he progressed to Marischal College, at the University of Aberdeen. There, in 1898, he took his medical degree with honours and received the Anderson Travelling Fellowship, which enabled him to work for a year at the Leipzig Institute of Physiology.

He was appointed Demonstrator of Physiology at the London Hospital Medical School in 1899 and, by 1902, he was Lecturer in Biochemistry. That same year he was awarded the McKinnon Research Studentship of the Royal Society, which he held until 1903 when, at the young age of 27, he became Professor of Physiology at the Western Reserve University in Cleveland, Ohio.

In 1903 he married his second cousin, Mary Watson McWalter, in the Church of Scotland, Paisley.

In 1918 he was appointed to the Chair of Physiology in Toronto, where he met Canadian, Dr Frederick Banting. Together they made a special study of diabetes and in 1923 John McLeod and Frederick Banting were jointly awarded the Nobel Prize for Physiology, as co-discoverers of Insulin.

Professor Macleod returned to Aberdeen in 1928 and was elected Regius Professor of Physiology and also Consultant to the Rowett Institute for Animal Nutrition. He remained there, even while suffering failing health, until his untimely death in 1935. He was survived by his widow, Mary, who died in Aberdeen in 1940. They did not have any children.

John McLeod held Honorary Doctorates from the Universities of Toronto, Cambridge, Aberdeen and Pennsylvania, plus many other honours which were bestowed upon him. He was a prolific writer of books and monographs on his work and research.

John Macleod and Frederick Banting shared their Nobel prize money with two of their colleagues (Dr Charles Best and Dr James Collip) who were deeply involved in the research project. All financial proceeds of the Insulin Patent were given to the British Medical Research Council for the encouragement of research.

So for a brief time Keith nurtured a future genius.

Nobel Medal

Manse

Former Free Church

WILLIAM GORDON MACPHERSON
'THE MAESTRO'
1888 - 1977

William Gordon Macpherson was born in Mulben in 1888, the son of John Macpherson, who farmed at Achlochrach, Glenrinnes. It was there, in 1867, that John Macpherson laid the foundations of the now world-famous herd of Aberdeen Angus cattle.

The family moved to the Mains of Mulben in 1888 and kept on the farms of Achlochrach and Achbreck for the breeding of sheep.

William received his education at Boharm School, Mulben, and Keith Grammar School. When his father died in 1921, William took over the farm and the herd of 'Blackskins'. Prior to that he had been a lieutenant in the Gordon Highlanders during World War I.

He became a prominent exporter, buying bulls at Perth sales and shipping them to Argentina. His knowledge and expertise were so respected that he was known as, 'The Maestro', and was much sought after as a judge at shows at both national and international levels. He was judge three times at The Great Palermo Show at Buenos Aires.

William G. Macpherson

At a local level he was President of the Aberdeen Angus Cattle Society and vice-chairman of the Banffshire Conservative and Unionist Association. He was a senior elder of Boharm Church, was active in community work and had long service with the local district council.

In the 1940's period one bull, from the herd at Mains of Mulben, was extra special and named 'Mulben Embassy'. It had a huge impact on the development of the breed in New Zealand, and later in Australia, and today, in the 21st century, that influence is still carried on world wide.

William Gordon Macpherson (The Maestro) retired in the 1960's and, in 1977 he died. His son, George Innes Macpherson, a veterinary surgeon, took over the running of the farm, until he, too, retired in the 1990's.

Then in the next generation, George's son, Innes Gordon Macpherson, took up the reins and in time, it is hoped, that his son, David, will carry on the original work of John MacPherson, who began the dynasty of the internationally famous Aberdeen Angus Cattle (Blackskins).

**George Macpherson
judging at Keith Show**

**George at
Mains of Mulben**

**Khartoum of Ballindalloch
another champion bull from Mains of Mulben**

GEORGE McWILLIE
1802 – 1885

George McWillie was born on 25th February 1802, at Cachenhead farm on Drummuir Estate, and was baptised in Botriphnie Church. His parents were William McWillie, wheelwright, and Isobel (nee Shearer).

At the age of 24, George began to keep notes, a brief summary of events, starting with 1826 then 1828, 1829 and 1830. In 1831 he adopted a more

Cachenhead

detailed style, by first recording events, then writing a monthly summary. He continued until his last surviving child, Jean, died aged 46. Thus he kept a detailed diary of working life in the area for a full 50 years.

George lived for a further 9 years, dying at Ardgaithney on 27th May 1885, and his wife Betty survived him by 19 years. Both are buried in Botriphnie Churchyard. George was well known locally for his knowledge in farming and keen business acumen, as well as having an interest in the well being of his fellow men.

Extracts from his diaries were reproduced in 'The Banffshire Herald' from 1997 to 1999. (See www.kadhg.org.uk)

"July 1853. The Nonintrusion Kirk the 1st, all split and rent, no building for the past 7 days, I doubt built on sand, I doubt its giving the people more trouble nor the preaching. Amen, The Nonintrusion Church condemned to be taken out at the foundation. The foundation deepened thirty inches and planking 3 inch thick laid in the bottom and was all built but one gavel top, the people like to eat thair thoumbs."

**Botriphnie
Free Church
at Woodend**

"June 1859. The new square at Ardbrack begun to build the 6th and the old house or castle dung down at this time, it is not known whean built or whom built, it was used the past 24 years for a threshing mill."

"New Square at Ardbrack", now Drummuir Home Farm

"Tuesday the 3rd October 1871, dray, fair day, east wind, about 15 caravans passed here for Keith with 4 elephants drawing 2 carriages, some verry fine horses."

Ardgaithney

ALEXANDER W. MAIR
1875 – 1928

Alexander William Mair was born on 9th June 1875, one of eight of a family to Charles Mair, merchant, Deerhill, Grange, and his wife Mary (nee Robertson). Five of the brothers went on to graduate with first-class honours in Classics at Aberdeen University. John trained as a minister and a headmaster. James and Gilbert rose to be headmasters. Robert became a Director of Education in Lanarkshire, and Alexander, a professor of Greek.

Alexander was educated at Crossroads School in Grange and Keith Public School. After leaving Keith aged fourteen, he graduated four years later from Aberdeen University. From there he proceeded to Gonville and Caius College, Cambridge where he won the Craven Scholarship, the highest possible award.

In 1898 he was appointed Assistant Professor of Greek at Aberdeen University, and the following year, aged only 24, to a similar post in Edinburgh, the youngest ever to hold the position.

He had a tragic death at his home on 13th November 1928, when fire destroyed his study, and it is believed he had been overcome by smoke inhalation. He left a widow and twelve children, the youngest only one month old. His untimely death robbed the country of a classical genius.

Gonville and Caius College, Cambridge,

HESIOD

THE POEMS AND FRAGMENTS

DONE INTO ENGLISH PROSE
WITH INTRODUCTION AND APPENDICES

BY

A. W. MAIR, M.A. (ABERD. ET CANTAB.)
PROFESSOR OF GREEK IN EDINBURGH UNIVERSITY
SOMETIME FELLOW OF GONVILLE AND CAIUS COLLEGE
CAMBRIDGE

OXFORD
AT THE CLARENDON PRESS
1908

Keith Public School

JOHN MAIR
1863 -1951

John Mair was born on 30th June 1863, the eldest member of the distinguished Mair family of Deerhill, Grange. He was educated at Crossroads, Grange school and Keith Public School. He entered Aberdeen University in 1880 as a first bursar and, being the most successful student of the year, was awarded the Town Council Gold Medal. He graduated with a first class honours degree in Classics.

John trained for the ministry at Edinburgh University, where he was recognised as one of the university's foremost scholars in Hebrew. He was assistant at the university to the Professor of Oriental Languages. In 1887 he became Assistant Minister at Nairn, a post he held for four years. As no full time ecclesiastical positions were vacant, in 1895 he was appointed headmaster of Keith Public School, renamed Keith Grammar School during his term of office.

In 1907 his dream was finally fulfilled and he became Minister of Spynie, a charge he held for almost forty years, during which time he was well respected in both the Parish and Presbytery of Spynie. Rev. John Mair died on Christmas Day 1951.

Keith Grammar School

Spynie Kirk

STANLEY MARK
1919 – 2001

Stanley Mark was born in November 1919, the second son of Alexander and Isabella Mark, and was one of six children. Having been a member of The Boys Brigade as a youth, he went on to become an officer. Following a short time in the Territorial Army, he joined the 1st Gordon Highlanders and during WWII served in the Middle East, North Africa and in North West Europe, before being wounded and discharged on health grounds.

He returned to Newmill, and to farming. Later he married Daphne Lowe and had four children. Over many years he played an active part in the community, serving on the Village Hall Committee, the War Memorial Committee, as a District Councillor and as a Justice of the Peace. He had a keen interest in local history and was often sought out by those researching family history with a Newmill connection. Stanley continued in farming until his death on 23rd August 2001.

Newmill Hall, Keith   I. M. Lawrence, Stationer, Keith

·MARKS · LANE·

Newmill War Memorial

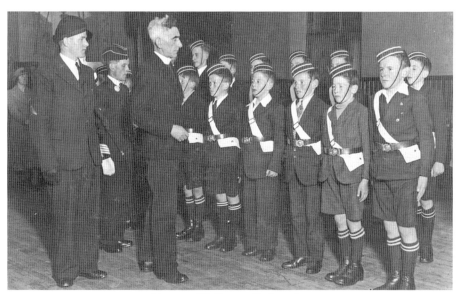

Newmill Boys Brigade

WILLIAM MITCHELL K.C.
1872 – 1937

William Mitchell was born in Mid Street, Keith on 8th October 1872, son of George Mitchell and Isabella (nee Burgess). Educated at Keith Public School, he graduated from Aberdeen University in Arts in 1893.

He furthered his education at Edinburgh University, as a Vans Dunlop Scholar in Scots Law and Conveyancing and gained an LLB. He held the post of Examiner in Legal Degrees at both Aberdeen and Edinburgh Universities and, in 1897, was called to the Scottish Bar.

In 1919, he became a King's Counsellor, having served as an Advocate-Depute for many years.

Mr Mitchell took a keen interest in politics and, on four occasions, stood as a Parliamentary candidate. In 1922 he stood as the National Liberal candidate in Kincardine and Western Aberdeenshire. In 1923 and 1924 he was the Liberal candidate in Peebles and Southern Midlothian. His final attempt to enter Westminster was in 1929 for Edinburgh North. He was unsuccessful on all four occasions.

In 1930 he was appointed Sheriff Substitute of Roxburgh, Berwick and Selkirk. That same year he published a book 'Prince Charles Edward Stewart and the Rising of 1745'.

William Mitchell was a Council member of Keith Grammar School Former Pupils' Association.

He died at his home Abbothills, Galashiels on 22nd February 1937, leaving behind his widow, Kathryn (nee Brammer).

Mid Street 1890's

Prince Charles Edward Stewart
of Scotland
And the Rising of 1745

BY

WILLIAM MITCHELL

EDINBURGH AND GLASGOW
WILLIAM HODGE & COMPANY, LIMITED
1930

JAMES NAUGHTIE
1951 –

James Naughtie, born 9th August 1951, was educated at Rothiemay Primary, where his father was Headmaster, and Keith Grammar where he was School Captain and a member of the rugby and football teams.

He obtained his MA with Honours in English from Aberdeen University and won a Scholarship to Syracuse University in New York, resulting in a further Degree.

James returned to Scotland and began a career in journalism as a trainee reporter with the Aberdeen 'Press & Journal'. He then moved to Edinburgh where he joined 'The Scotsman' specialising in political affairs. Having won a Lawrence Stern Fellowship, he spent two years working on 'The Washington Post' and then, in 1984, he joined 'The Guardian' as chief political correspondent.

He branched into Broadcasting (in 1986 'The Week in Westminster' and in 1988 'The World at One' on Radio 4) and the making of documentaries. His love of music and literature came to the fore when presenting programmes such as 'BBC Proms' and 'Bookclub'.

He married Eleanor Updale in 1986 at Westminster in London and they have three children. They live in Edinburgh and London.

In 1991, he was voted Radio Personality of the Year in the Sony Radio Awards. He has been conferred with an Hon. LLD by the Universities of Aberdeen, St Andrews and Stirling, and an Hon. DLitt from the Universities of Glasgow Caledonian and Edinburgh Napier, and in 2008 he was appointed Chancellor of Stirling University.

Mr Naughtie is a regular contributor to journals, magazines and newspapers and has several publications to his credit. Among them are: 'The Rivals' (2001), 'The Accidental American' (2004) and 'The Making of Music' (2007).

Rothiemay Primary School

He is currently a presenter on the BBC Radio 4 'Today 'programme and in 2014 will also be part of Radio Scotland's 'Good Morning, Scotland' team in the run-up to the Independence referendum.

Keith Grammar School until 1965

Keith Grammar School from 1965

JOHN OGILVIE
1580 - 1615
Written in collaboration with the late Mary Roche

John Ogilvie was born at Drum of Keith in 1580, the eldest son of Walter Ogilvie, a Calvinist and local Laird.

When he was 12 – 13 years of age he was sent to Europe to finish his education. He was enrolled in 1592 at the University of Helmstedt in Brunswick, Germany. Four years later he was admitted to the Scots College at Louvain, near Brussels. It is believed that between 1592 and 1596 he became a Catholic. In 1598 he left Louvain and went to Olmutz in Moravia. He requested to be admitted to the Society of Jesus and made his profession as a Jesuit in 1601. In accordance with the custom of the Order he was ordained a Priest in 1610 in Paris at the age of 30 years.

In 1613, at his own request, he returned to his homeland, Scotland, which at that time was in the grip of the post-Reformation persecution of Catholics. After a brief visit to France to consult with the Superior of the Scottish mission he returned to Scotland. He conducted worship in secret for a year until he was betrayed by a 'friend' to the authorities on the 14th October, 1614. As a result he was imprisoned and subjected to brutal and vile torture but he never revealed names of the Catholics he knew, instead he showed great stoicism and fortitude in the adversity which had befallen him.

After many days of argument and continual torture in Edinburgh he was condemned as a traitor. On the 10th March, 1615 he was hanged at Glasgow Cross and buried as a felon in a grave to the North of Glasgow Cathedral.

In the 17th century he was declared the Venerable John Ogilvie and in 1929 he was beatified – and became the Blessed John Ogilvie.

It was not until 17th October 1976 that John Ogilvie was canonised by Pope Paul VI in Rome. There was great rejoicing in Keith and Glasgow, the latter because that was where the 'miraculous cure of John Fagan' had taken place. An aircraft full of Keith people flew to Rome for the canonisation ceremony. Many were dressed in the newly-designed Ogilvie tartan, which was a product of the local Laidlaws, Seafield Wool Mill.

A statue of St John Ogilvie, sculpted by Basil Robinson, a monk of Pluscarden Abbey, was placed in the left-hand niche at the entrance to St Thomas' Chapel and is dedicated to reconciliation, not to the memory of injustice. Inside there is a small St John Ogilvie chapel for meditation and prayer. The statue in the Chapel was created by Anne Davidson, a former pupil of the Sacred Heart School, Queen's Cross, Aberdeen. A new painting of the Martyr by Peter Howson has been unveiled and was placed in St Andrews Cathedral, Glasgow in 2011. After centuries of deliberation the Blessed John Ogilvie, native of Keith, was canonised – Scotland's first post-Reformation Saint .

"In all that concerns the King, I will be slavishly obedient: if any attack his temporal power, I shall shed my last drop of blood for him. But in things of spiritual jurisdiction which a King unjustly seizes I cannot and must not obey." John Ogilvie 1615

University of Helmstedt

**Statue in
St Thomas niche**

St Thomas Chapel, Keith

DR NEIL PRATT
1938 – 2006

Neil Pratt was born on 6th December 1938, the third son of George and Lizzie Pratt of Pratt's Pharmacy, Mid Street, Keith. He showed an early interest in astronomy and constructed his own telescopes from cardboard.

**Pratt Family home
Drum Road, Keith**

He was Dux of Mathematics and of Keith Grammar School in 1956 and went on to further his education at Edinburgh University, gaining a first class honours degree and a PhD in Physics.

His first position was with The Royal Greenwich Observatory at Herstmonceux Castle in Sussex. Dr Pratt progressed to Jodrell Bank, Cheshire and it is reported that, not only did he design a computer programme to interpret the 21-inch plates from the Royal Observatory, he built the actual computer. Dr Pratt and his wife returned to his hometown of Keith to retire but sadly he died suddenly on 30th November 2006.

**Keith Grammar School class photograph
Neil Pratt back row extreme left.**

126

Jodrell Bank

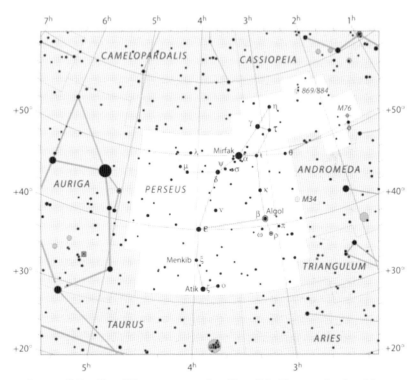

One of Dr Pratt's papers dealt with the polarization of starlight from Constellation Perseus

JOHN RIPLEY VC
1867 - 1933

John Ripley was born on 30th August 1867 in Land Sreet to Joseph and Margaret (nee Castles). He was educated at Keith Primary School (Green School) and Keith Grammar School. He left school at the age of 13 and was employed in the Spinning Department of Isla Bank Mills. Two years later John and his brother moved to Montrose where they trained as slaters. On completing his apprenticeship, John moved to work in St Andrews where he joined the Volunteer and Territorial unit of the Black Watch. He married Jane Laing in 1895.

When World War I began in 1914, John was Recruiting Sergeant at St Andrews but such was his patriotism that at the late age of 47 he enlisted with the 1st Black Watch.

On 9th May 1915, during the battle of Aubers Ridge in North East France, he led his section on an assault at Rue du Bois and was the first man to ascend the enemy parapet. He directed those following to gaps in the barbed wire entanglement, all the while under heavy fire from the enemy. He and eight soldiers established themselves, blocking both flanks and arranging firing positions which he continued to defend until all his men had fallen and he himself had been badly wounded. John had been shot in the leg and a piece of shrapnel had entered his forehead, passing under the skin to emerge behind his left ear.

Afterwards he said he had only done his duty, adding modestly that he was one of the lucky ones as there were many other brave fellows who hadn't survived.

On the 24th July 1915 'The Banffshire Herald' carried the following report: ***"The Victoria Cross has been awarded to Corporal John Ripley of the 1st Black Watch, a native of Keith"***. The newspaper goes on to describe his conspicuous bravery at Rue du Bois. Newspapers in St Andrews also feted the hero's return. It was reported elsewhere that John was probably the first member of Kitchener's Army to receive the coveted award, which is held in the Black Watch Museum in Balhousie Castle, Perth.

Promoted to Sergeant, John Ripley was invalided home but later returned to active duty. After the War ended and normal life resumed, John became a member of the United Services Association and The British Legion and chairman of the St Andrews Branch of The Comrades, which later merged with The British Legion.

In 1933, at the age of 66, John suffered an accident when he fell from a ladder in St Andrews, which resulted in his death from injuries and so ended the heroic life of John Ripley, one of the oldest soldiers to receive the VC. He was buried with honours in the Upper Largo cemetery in Fife.

Black Watch Red Hackle

Sgt J. Ripley VC and Sgt Mjr F. Barter VC at their investiture

Gravestone at Upper Largo

GEORGE SELLAR VC
1850 –1889

George Sellar was born in 1850 in Wellington Terrace, Fife-Keith. About 1869 he enlisted in the 72nd Regiment. On 14th December 1879, while serving in Afghanistan with the 72nd Regiment during the Second Afghan War, Lance Corporal Sellar led an attack on Asmai Heights, outside Kabul. During the fierce battle he was severely wounded but his bravery had not gone unnoticed and he was awarded the Victoria Cross for displaying gallantry in the field of battle.

The citation in the London Gazette 18th October 1881 reads:

"For conspicuous gallantry displayed by him at the assault on the Asmai Heights, round Kabul, on the 14th December 1879, in having in a marked manner led the attack, under a heavy fire, and dashing on in front of the party up a slope, engaged in a desperate conflict with an Afghan who sprang out to meet him. In this encounter Lance Corporal Sellar was severely wounded."

In 1881 the 72nd Regiment amalgamated with the 78th Regiment to become the 1st Battalion Seaforth Highlanders. By 1882 George had been promoted to the rank of Sergeant.

The Battalion was sent to Egypt during the Anglo-Egyptian War of 1882 and was involved in the battle of Tel-el-Kebir. In 1887 he was appointed Sergeant Instructor of the Lairg Company of the 1st Sutherland and Caithness Highland Rifle Volunteers.

Sergeant Sellar died on 1st November 1889 and was laid to rest in Lairg cemetery in Sutherland. His Victoria Cross can be seen at the Highlanders Museum, Fort George, Ardersier.

Citadel, Kandahar 1881

George Sellar's Medals left to right:

Victoria Cross
Afghanistan Medal with clasps: Piewar Kotal, Charasiah, Kabul, Kandahar
Kabul-Kandahar Star
Egypt Medal with clasp: Tel-el-Kebir
Khedive Star 1882

JAMES SIMMIE SHARP
1825 - 1909

James Simmie Sharp was born on the 12th March 1825, on the farm of Parroch, Rothiemay to William and Margaret (nee Redford).

He received his early education under the tutelage of a Mr Rae at Morningside school, Rothiemay and then at the Parish School with headmaster William Webster. He then attended Aberdeen University and, after qualifying, taught for a spell at Cairney School. In November 1847, he became master at the Free Church School at Woodhead, Fyvie and afterwards at the Fyvie Public School. He retired in November 1888 having spent 41 years in the educational service of that Parish and received many accolades plus an illuminated address.

On his retirement, James returned to Rothiemay and acquired the properties of Whitestones and Upper Woodside. In 1889 he was elected to the school board in Rothiemay, a post he held until he resigned in 1907 due to ill health.

There is a curious link here with Robert Laidlaw who had arrived in 1882 to work the wool mill at the Isla Bridge adjacent to Whitestones and of which James was now the owner.

The ex-schoolmaster was notoriously stingy with regards to money; so when Robert Laidlaw asked him for assistance in modernising the mill to keep up with current trends, James Sharp declined, even though Robert offered a higher rent. This action was to be of great benefit to the neighbouring town of Keith as Robert Laidlaw moved his business there in 1901 and established a very successful wool mill which lasted for a century. A sad loss for Rothiemay but a huge benefit to Keith as it was to be one of the mainstays of that town's economy.

James Simmie Sharp did not forget his parish School and upon his death in 1909 he left trust settlements of two bursaries (the Sharpe bursaries) to the annual value of £30 each, tenable at Aberdeen University for four years by Arts students of Rothiemay and Fyvie Schools. He also left four bursaries of £5 each tenable at Rothiemay Public School.

His unusual middle name of Simmie came about because the minister of Rothiemay for a time was the Rev. Dr James Simmie, an eminent and greatly respected man. Many parents, when having their child baptised by the Rev. Dr Simmie, gave their offspring the middle name of Simmie, as a mark of respect and honour. Were they perhaps secretly hoping that the Minister's academic abilities might brush off on their beloved child?

James Simmie Sharp died at Whitestones on 27th October 1909 and was buried in Rothiemay Kirkyard.

Bridge of Isla and Whitestones

Pupils at Rothiemay School

BRIDGETON of ISLA ROTHIEMAY

ROBERT SIM
1793 – 1866

Robert Sim, son of John Sim, shoemaker, and Jane (nee McKachan) was born in Keith on 11th November 1793. Robert was well known for his writing of articles for local newspapers and books on antiquarian and historical topics, such as 'The Legends of Strathisla', 'Walk from Keith to Rothiemay', 'Old Keith' and 'A Stroll to Cairnie'. He was also an accomplished poet and was heavily involved in local amateur dramatics.

He kept an extensive library, which was open to members of the public.

As well as his literary achievements, Robert Sim was widely known for his kindly disposition and willingness to join in any charitable undertaking.

Robert's brother, William, had been First Assistant in the Office of the Chief Secretary to the Governor of Malta. A new house on the site of the family home on the corner of Reidhaven Square and Mid Street, was built by William with design input by Robert. It was named Malta House.

Robert Sim, who had been predeceased by his wife Marjory Sinclair, died on 12th August 1866, aged 72, and was buried in Ruthven Churchyard, Cairnie, the ancestral parish of the Sim family.

Keith Square looking towards the Balloch 1837

Robert Sim

LEGENDS

OF

STRATHISLA, INVERNESS-SHIRE,

AND

STRATHBOGIE:

WITH AN APPENDIX.

THIRD EDITION:

TO WHICH IS ADDED

A WALK FROM KEITH TO ROTHIEMAY,

BY THE SAME AUTHOR.

OLD KEITH:

LOVE OF HOME, SCENERY, EVENTS, &c.;

AND

A STROLL TO CAIRNIE.

& SON,

BY THE AUTHOR OF "LEGENDS OF STRATHISLA," &c.

WITH

INTRODUCTORY REMARKS.

BY

ALEXANDER SIMPSON
1892 – 1973

Alexander Simpson was born at 2 Nelson Terrace, Fife-Keith on 11th October 1892. He was one of a family of nine children to William Simpson, manure manufacturer, and his wife Mary Martin. He was always interested in sport and while a pupil at Keith Grammar School played in the school football team. Whilst still a scholar he was approached several times to play in the senior Keith Football team and often recalled that fact with great pride.

At the age of 18 he left Keith to work in Malaya as a rubber planter. During internment by the Japanese in the Second World War he would often recall the days of his youth in Keith.

He amassed a fortune from his rubber plantation and in dealings in the Stock Exchange.

Alexander Simpson retired to Scotland to live with his sister in Fochabers and died, aged 80 on the 12th March 1973.

The Simpson Trust was set up from a large sum of money bequeathed in his will for the promotion of sport for the young people of Keith, with a particular emphasis on football.

The Trust acquired land between Westerton Road and Drum Road for the construction of the Simpson Park comprising two football pitches, a pavilion and associated facilities. The Alexander Simpson Community Park was officially opened on 11th October 1998 and is used extensively by local schools for sports and inter-school competitions. The pavilion is also home to the Sunshine Developmental Playgroup.

The Ground is used by other sporting organisations, including the local running club. Simpson Park is fully enclosed and is a convenient neutral venue for regional sporting competitions. Local Keith football clubs, such as Islavale in the SJFA North Division, and Ugie United in the Welfare League, make use of the football pitches for their matches. Many other local sports have benefited from the provisions of the Simpson Trust.

ISLAVALE J.F.C
WELCOMES YOU
TO
SIMPSON PARK

Islavale entertain Portgordon at Simpson Park

No 2 Nelson Terrace

Spectators at Simpson Park

ISOBEL LIND SMITH
1921-1979

Isobel Lind Smith was born in Keith on the 10th October 1921. Sadly her father Dr James Lind Smith died just before her birth. Her mother Sarah Isabella Smith then stayed on with her parents who lived in Craighill, Seafield Avenue

Isobel received her education at Keith Primary School and Keith Grammar School.

After her schooling was completed she left home to train as a primary school teacher. When qualified, she came back during the Second World War to teach in the recently opened Keith Senior Primary School ('The New School' 1939-2010) and remained in that teaching post for 15 years. She was also a Sunday School teacher at the Keith North Church.

As time moved forward she felt that her vocation was to be a Missionary and so in 1958 she took up a position at the Kapeni College in Blantyre, Nyasaland (now Malawi). In 1969 she was promoted to Principal of that College.

At Kapeni College she noticed a young boy who showed great academic potential and, ever anxious for her pupils, she thought the best place for him to further his education was at her home town's Grammar School. She made the necessary arrangements and Vincent D'Mello arrived in Keith and quickly settled into school routine. In time he went to Aberdeen University and graduated in

Keith Senior Primary School

138

Biochemistry He did not let his mentor down and went on to greater works in Ontario, Canada .

When her term of office was over at Kapeni College she returned to begin work as Assistant Secretary for the Overseas Council at the Church of Scotland in Edinburgh

On holiday in 1979 she visited Keith to stay with relatives. During this time a dreadful accident occurred when her dress caught fire and she was badly burned. She was rushed to Woodend Hospital, Aberdeen but tragically died as a result of her extensive injuries.

When her will was read it was found that she had bequeathed to Keith North Church the sum of £20,000. After careful deliberation it was decided to replace the organ and restore the frontage of the Church with her generous legacy.

Isobel and visiting Red Cross official at Kapeni

A Thanksgiving Service in her memory was held in 1981 and a memorial plaque now hangs within the North Church.

Although her life was cut short at the age of 57, Isobel Smith left a wonderful legacy of a life in which she had accomplished so many good works.

TO THE GLORY OF GOD
AND IN GRATEFUL MEMORY OF
ISOBEL LIND SMITH.
PRINCIPAL OF KAPENI COLLEGE.
BLANTYRE, MALAWI
1969 – 1974
AND A MEMBER OF THIS CONGREGATION.
WHOSE GENEROUS BEQUEST
HAS MADE IT POSSIBLE
TO REPLACE THE ORGAN
AND HAVE THE STONEWORK
OF THE CHURCH RESTORED.

SEPTEMBER 1981.

North Kirk

139

GEORGE STABLES   DCM   MM
1899 - 1981

George Stables was born in
Keith in 1899 and received his
education at Keith Primary
School and Keith Grammar
School.

When World War I broke
out in 1914, George overstated
his age and volunteered for the
6th Gordon Highlanders. He was
accepted, but later when his
correct age was discovered, he
was discharged and had to wait
until he was legally eighteen
years old before he was allowed
to re-join the Regiment.

He was officially called up,
aged 18, in 1918. Within six
months he found himself on the
battlefield at Avesnes-le-Sechvin
where his bravery was noted
and he was awarded the
Distinguished Conduct Medal.
Later, in the same year, he was
again in the thick of the fighting
at the battle of Famas in France
and this time he was awarded
the Military Medal.

This gallant soldier, still only eighteen years old and the recipient of
two medals was a sterling example of a 6th Gordon Highlander. By the
time the war ended he had been promoted to Sergeant and chose to
remain in the Army for a further two years.

On his return to his hometown of Keith, Sergeant Stables found
employment with Banff County Council, Roads Department and remained
in their employ for 43 years until retiring in 1965.

Mr Stables married a local girl and together they raised a family of
three sons and one daughter.

Mr. Stables was a founder member of the Keith British Legion,
served as a Committee Member and Vice-President and also paid regular
and popular visits to those members who were sick or in hospital. In 1974
he was presented with a certificate of Life Membership and a Gold Badge
in honour and recognition of his services to the Royal British Legion.

This double medal holder died on 11th October 1981 leaving the
proud record of a heroic and brave 6th Gordon Highlander.

140

Distinguished Conduct Medal

S/22589 Sjt. G. STABLES 6/7th Bn. TF (Keith)
For conspicuous gallantry and ability in
command of a daylight reconnoitring patrol
north of Avesnes-le-Sec on the 14th October
1918. He led a patrol to a position well
within the enemy lines, where it came under
very heavy machine-gun fire at close range.
He then proceeded to withdraw his patrol in
accordance with the orders he had received.
Finding his retreat cut off, he remained
within the enemy's lines till nearly dusk
when, by a skilful manoeuvre , he succeeded
in getting back all his patrol except two,
killed. He attended to all the wounded, saw
them safely back to our lines, and was the
last to leave.

Military Medal

JOHN STRACHAN
1862 – 1907

John Strachan was born on 31st January 1862 the only son of James and Ann Strachan (nee Kerr), who farmed The Brae, Keith. Educated at Keith Public School, at just 15 years of age he went to Aberdeen University and in 1881 graduated MA with First Class Honours in Classics.

Having won the Simpson Prize for Greek, the Seafield Gold Medal for English and the Fullerton Scholarship, he won the Ferguson Scholarship in 1882 and in the following year he was the first Scot to win the Porson university scholarship at Cambridge.

He showed exceptional brilliance and following studies at Jena University in Germany he graduated from Cambridge University in 1885. During that summer, at the young age of 23, he was appointed Professor of Greek at Owens College, Manchester University, being the youngest Professor in Great Britain at that time. He later incorporated Comparative Philology, which is the study of the relationship between languages.

In 1886 he married Mina Grant, a daughter of his former headmaster, Dr James Grant of Keith and they had six daughters and two sons.

Professor Strachan was a recognised authority on Old Irish, Sanskrit, Gaelic and Welsh and was a great inspiration to his students. It was reported that 'duties of profession and study of languages were his hobby as well as his work'. In 1900 he was awarded LLD from Aberdeen University in recognition of his work at Victoria University, Manchester.

He wrote 'Selections from the Old Irish Glosses' and, in conjunction with Dr Whitley Stokes, the 'Thesaurus Palaeo–Hibernicus'. His last work 'An Introduction to Early Welsh' was incomplete on his death. He had caught a chill which developed into pneumonia. He died in 1907 aged 45 at his home in Prestwich, Manchester.

There is a John Strachan Lecture held annually (usually in March) at Aberdeen University when eminent Celtic scholars deliver lectures, among them many prominent Professors. These lectures are later published in pamphlet form and are available from the School of Celtic Studies at Aberdeen University.

Brae of Montgrew Farm

John Owens Building, Manchester University

THESAURUS PALAEOHIBERNICUS

A COLLECTION OF OLD-IRISH GLOSSES
SCHOLIA PROSE AND VERSE

ISABELLA TAYLOR
1875 - 1957

Isabella Taylor (nee Hay) was born at Oakenknowes in Grange on 31st January 1875. She was a Primary School teacher until her marriage in 1907 to Dr James Taylor of Ugie House, a local medical practitioner who later served as Provost of Keith from 1913 to 1919.

During WWI Isabella manned a canteen for troops at the army camp at Maisley, Keith and was awarded the MBE for her war work.

In 1924 Isabella and Mrs Eleonora Gray, 101 Mid Street, were the first women ever to be elected to Keith Town Council.

In 1929 she successfully contested Keith Landward and was elected to the County Council, later being appointed Vice Chairman of Public Health. She also served on the Education Committee, the Public Assistance Committee and the Coal Board.

Mrs Isabella Taylor served on the Advisory Committee of the Unemployment Association of Aberdeenshire, Banffshire and Kincardineshire. She was appointed a Justice of the Peace in 1942 and was also an Honorary President of St Rufus Woman's Guild.

Mrs Taylor died at Ugie House, Keith on 29th May 1957. Her son, Dr J. Lennel Taylor, was a Doctor in Keith for many years.

In 1958 a plaque was unveiled in St Rufus Church to honour Isabella Taylor and her husband Dr James Taylor, both worthy and respected citizens of Keith.

In 1929 Mrs Taylor defeated sitting County Councillor ex-Provost John Kynoch in Keith Landward.

Banff County Council Coat of Arms

Ugie House, Church Road

3/6th Gordons at Maisley Camp, Keith

JAMES TAYLOR
1798 – 1882

James Taylor was born on 9th September 1798 in Mid Street, Keith, in a house on the site later occupied by the Keith Municipal Institute. He was the eldest of six brothers and three sisters. His parents were James Taylor, originally from Rothiemay, a merchant of long standing in Mid Street, and his wife, Mary Wright, from Whitehouse, Aberlour. James, the father, spent the last 27 years of his life in the West Indies as factor of a large estate on the island of Grenada.

Young James' early education took place in Keith and he was then placed into the care of his maternal uncle, a solicitor in Glasgow. After further schooling in Edinburgh, he graduated from Aberdeen University and then joined the Royal Navy.

In 1824 he entered the naval medical service and served on the West African coast, in the West Indies, Canada and the Mediterranean, where he was Medical Officer to the Commander-in-Chief, Mediterranean Fleet. He spent six years as Head of the Naval Hospital in Georgetown, Ascension Island and was appointed Deputy Inspector-General of Fleets and Hospitals before retiring from the Navy in 1863. He then gained his MD in 1865.

Dr Taylor never married and amassed a considerable fortune. He bought the estate of Greenskares near Banff for £10,000. Later, in 1875, he presented the estate to the University of Aberdeen to fund the Greenskares Bursaries in Arts. This provided bursaries of £30 to be granted to youths born in or educated in Banffshire. For the last six years of his life Dr Taylor was in poor health and confined to bed at his home in Portobello near Edinburgh, where he died on 9th July 1882.

He had also presented £500 to provide prizes for the pupils of the Keith Schools. He gave amounts of £1,200 and £1,500 to be administered by the Minister and Kirk Session of Keith for the poor of the parish who were not already in receipt of parochial relief. Sums of £350 and £300 were given to provide annual long-service awards of £12 and £10 to agricultural workers and domestic servants. An amount of £350 provided for an annual prize of £12 for the best shot in the county with a military rifle. The residue of his estate (£3,500) was gifted to Turner Memorial Hospital.

After his death a subscription raised £137:19s for a memorial and in 1885, a fountain of grey granite with five columns of pink and grey marble complete with four lion-head water spouts was erected in Reidhaven Square, Keith – this can be seen in old photographs of the Square. In 1933, the fountain was moved to its present position in front of St Rufus Gardens, directly across from St Rufus Church. The inscription opposite pays tribute to this illustrious gentleman.

Georgetown with the Hospital to the right

146

TO THE MEMORY OF
JAMES TAYLOR ESQUIRE   M.D.

DEPUTY INSPECTOR GENERAL OF HOSPITALS AND FLEETS. BORN IN KEITH   1798, DIED IN PORTOBELLO 1882.   IN RECOGNITION OF A LONG HONOURABLE AND WELL SPENT LIFE; IN GRATITUDE FOR HIS MUNIFICENT LEGACY TO THE TURNER MEMORIAL HOSPITAL; FOR HIS DISINTERESTED KINDNESS IN ESTABLISHING THE GREENSKARES BURSARIES, AND FOR MANY OTHER GENEROUS AND CHARITABLE BEQUESTS LEFT BY HIM TO HIS NATIVE PARISH AND TOWN.

THIS MONUMENT IS ERECTED BY HIS FELLOW TOWNSMEN. AD 1885

Old Barracks, Georgetown, Ascension Island

SIR THOMAS MURRAY TAYLOR
1897 – 1962

Thomas Murray Taylor was born 1897 in Keith, the son of John Taylor and his wife Jenny (nee Murray). He was educated at Keith Primary and Keith Grammar Schools.

He was Dux at Keith Grammar school in 1915 and was awarded every medal and distinction from the school. At Aberdeen University, where he studied as a Classical scholar reading ancient languages, he graduated with first class honours in 1919, receiving gold medals in Greek and Latin. Later that year he was awarded two Scholarships, namely the Fullerton and the Ferguson Classics. He decided to study Law and in 1922 graduated LLB.

He moved to Edinburgh to practise and while there was called to the Bar. In 1929 he was appointed HM Advocate Depute and, after he had been engaged in a number of notable trials, he became Senior Advocate Depute in 1934. The following year he returned to Aberdeen where he was appointed to the Chair of Law at Aberdeen University.

He was noted for the exceptional quality of his orations when promoting candidates for Honorary Degrees of Doctor of Laws. These addresses combined wisdom, learning, wit and understanding of human nature. As his career progressed he became Principal and Vice Chancellor of Aberdeen University in 1948, a popular decision in the city. When he presented Winston Churchill with his LLD in 1946, the former Prime Minister was so impressed with Thomas Taylor's address that he requested a copy be sent to him. This gift of oratory gained him national renown and books of his addresses to university students were published.

From 1945 to 1948 he held office as Sheriff of Renfrew and Argyll and over the years held many offices and commissions.

This distinguished man's educational honours are lengthy and his services recognised by many institutions. In 1944 he received a CBE and was created a KC in 1945. He was knighted in 1954 which was a great honour for him, his family, university and his home town of Keith.

Thomas Taylor won national recognition in his work for the Church of Scotland and, as a member of the executive committee of the World Council of Churches, represented the Kirk abroad. He believed in equal opportunities for all people and was at one time Chairman of the Inquiry into Crofting Conditions. Thomas Taylor had a great love of the North East of Scotland, for its culture, land and language and championed it at every opportunity.

He received a DD from Edinburgh University an LLD from Glasgow and St Andrews Universities. Sir Thomas was a Fellow of the Royal Society of Edinburgh and an Hon. Fellow of the Educational Institute of Scotland. In 1954 he was made a Commander of the Swedish Royal Order of the North Star.

Sir Thomas Taylor died on the 19 July 1962 and was buried in Keith Old Cemetery. He was survived by Lady Taylor and a son and daughter.

Thomas Taylor

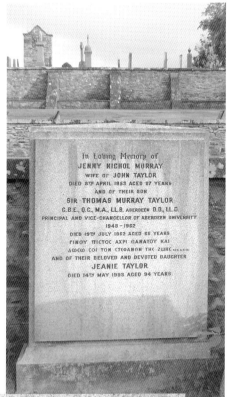

In Loving Memory of
JENNY NICHOL MURRAY
WIFE OF JOHN TAYLOR
DIED 8TH APRIL 1953 AGED 87 YEARS
AND OF THEIR SON
SIR THOMAS MURRAY TAYLOR
C.B.E., Q.C., M.A., LL.B. ABERDEEN D.D., LL.D
PRINCIPAL AND VICE-CHANCELLOR OF ABERDEEN UNIVERSITY
1948-1962
DIED 19TH JULY 1962 AGED 65 YEARS
ΓΙΝΟΥ ΠΙCΤΟC ΑΧΡΙ ΘΑΝΑΤΟΥ ΚΑΙ
ΔΩCΩ COI ΤΟΝ CΤΕΦΑΝΟΝ ΤΗC ΖΩΗC REV. 2.V.10.
AND OF THEIR BELOVED AND DEVOTED DAUGHTER
JEANIE TAYLOR
DIED 14TH MAY 1993 AGED 94 YEARS

ΓΙΝΟΥ ΠΙCΤΟC ΑΧΡΙ ΘΑΝΑΤΟΥ ΚΑΙ
ΔΩCΩ COI ΤΟΝ CΤΕΦΑΝΟΝ ΤΗC ΖΩΗC REV. 2.V.10.

Gravestone and detail in Greek (Rev. 2.10)

The Knowe, Taylor family home in Broomhill Road

MARGARET THOM
1884 – 1952
Contributed by the late Muriel Gray

Margaret Cruickshank was born at Ramsburn on 14th February 1884, youngest of eleven children. At the age of 22 she married Peter Thom in the Glenbarry Inn and they lived at Ternemny before moving to Inchdrewer, near Banff. Their final home was their cottage, The Firs, in Grange. They had two sons and two adopted sons and also gave a loving home to fourteen other children.

Margaret had a talent and a passion for writing, resulting in her having four books of prose and poetry published: 'Hamely Rhymes for Hamely Folk', 'The Patchwork Quilt', 'The Hearthrug' and finally 'Clippens'. She contributed weekly columns to the 'Banffshire Herald' under the penname 'M.T.'. These were widely read and especially appreciated by locals serving in the forces during World War II. She died on 10th May 1952 after a long illness and her well-attended funeral paid testimony to her popularity in the district.

RHYMIN' MEGGIE

Nae for me a wreath o' laurels,
Nor braw letters at my name;
I am only rhymin' Meggie,
In a puir and humble hame.

But oftimes I get a letter
That sets my heart aflame,
Tellin' me that in the "Herald"
My writing' brings a glint o' hame.

To some exile ower the watter.
Far frae a their kith an' kin;
Far frae whaur the heather's bloomin'
On the Knock , the Durn, the Binn.

So though I hae nae routh o' siller,
Nor braw letters at my name;
If I've cheered one Scottish exile,
I will not have rhymed in vain.

Margaret Thom outside The Firs, Grange

ANDREW THOMSON
c1838 – 1913

Andrew Thomson was born at Peterhead in c1838, son of Alexander Thomson and Christine (nee Anderson). He was educated at Peterhead Schools and, after reaching the leaving age, he was apprenticed to a carpenter in Aberdeen. Andrew, however, had a studious and enquiring mind .and began to attend evening classes. He later found employment with a firm of architects, Messrs Matthew and Mackenzie, as an Inspector of Works and in time was promoted to Chief Assistant to the company. During this period he trained several famous architects including Dr Marshall Mackenzie.

In 1865 he married Ann Martin, who was born in Drumoak. They had a family of three daughters and two sons. Isabella, the youngest daughter, was born in Keith. In 1876 he was appointed head architect of the Richmond and Gordon estates of Morayshire, Banffshire and Aberdeenshire and chose to live in Keith. The Haughs was the family home for a time and by 1901 they had moved to 5 Braco Street, Fife-Keith.

He immersed himself in local societies, becoming a founder member of Keith Field Club and the Mutual Improvement Society. Andrew, along with his friend Alexander Thurburn, Solicitor, spent time devising experiments to illustrate their weekly 'Select Lectures' on such diverse subjects as sight, sound, wireless telegraphy, photography and X-rays. They also spent a lot of time in the Keith Museum when it was in Chapel House and later when it transferred to the new Institute. Andrew was a Director of the Keith Institute Company Ltd. from its inception.

He was a staunch member of the South United Free Church (located at the junction of Chapel Street and Land Street). In 1901 he was presented with a planimeter and prismatic compass for the free help he had given in the refurbishment of the church and manse.

A great admirer of the astronomer James Ferguson FRS, he began to build an exact copy of an orrery from designs in Ferguson's 'Select Exercises' of 1780. It took him twelve years to complete the orrery and then he embarked on a replica of Ferguson's astronomical clock . Both were presented to Keith Grammar School in 1929 by Mrs Mary Hay, Andrew Thomson's daughter. These are still preserved in the school; a fitting tribute to a man who was dedicated to furthering knowledge and education.

Andrew Thomson died on 18 October 1913 and was buried in Broomhill Cemetery. As a mark of the esteem in which he was held, the Institute bell was tolled as the cortege made its way from Fife-Keith to Broomhill.

His daughter, Annie, married William Robb, Solicitor, whose name lives on in the business of Stephen and Robb, Solicitors, Mid Street, Keith.

Andrew Thomson

South United Free Church

Thomson Family

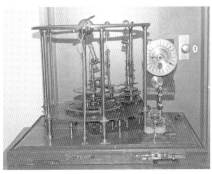

Orrery

Celestial Clock

REV. DR FORBES TOCHER MC
1885 – 1973

Forbes Scott Tocher was born in Whitehills in Banffshire on 9th February 1885, son of James and Elsie Tocher and was brought up by his grandparents.

Educated at Fordyce Academy, he graduated MA from Aberdeen University in 1906 and was awarded a BD from Edinburgh University in 1909. That same year he was ordained as a Missionary of the Church of Scotland and his calling took him to Ichang, China, where he served until the outbreak of World War I. He served in the Royal Artillery from 1916–1919, first as an enlisted gunner and later as a commissioned officer, and was awarded the Military Cross for his fearless determination and perseverance.

He then returned to Ichang, on the Yangtse River, and in 1928 was awarded the CBE in recognition of his part in the rescue of a Naval Officer at the mercy of Chinese river pirates.

An Honorary Doctor of Divinity was bestowed upon him by Aberdeen University in 1934. Dr Forbes was interned by the Japanese in a concentration camp in Shanghai for the duration of World War II. He later returned to his homeland and, from 1948 until his retirement to Cullen in 1955, he served as Minister of Botriphnie Parish Church. Mrs Joanna Forbes, his first wife, died in 1957 and they had one daughter, Agnes.

He married his second wife, Helen Wilson in 1965 after having been reunited in 1961. They had previously met in Ichang, where Miss Wilson had been a nurse at the Mission. Rev. Dr Tocher died on 15th August 1973 at Banff and was interred in Banff Cemetery.

MC

CBE

Tocher Terrace, Drummuir bears the name of this remarkable man.

Botriphnie Church christening
Mrs D. Hammond, Rev. Dr Tocher,
baby Linda Hammond and Mrs Joanna Tocher

DR ROBERT TURNER
1812 – 1877

Robert Turner was born in Elgin on 4th December 1812 and, after a highly successful university education, came to practise medicine in Keith in 1834. He was a well-respected and popular Doctor, who gave unstintingly of his time to his patients. He was appointed Examiner of Midwifery for Aberdeen University in 1876 and also served terms as President of North of Scotland Medical Association. Among other interests, he was Honorary President of Keith Literary Society, a position he held from its formation until his death.

He lived at Cuthil View, Land Street with his wife Agnes (nee Kynoch) and they had two daughters and five sons. One son, Dr Robert Shand Turner joined the practice in 1869 and between them they gave almost 100 years of service to the community. His main desire was to see the creation of a Cottage Hospital catering for Keith and the neighbouring district. He confided this to his friend, Mr William Longmore, a local benefactor, and in 1877, with much encouragement and financial support

Cuthil View

from various sources, a Committee was formed of interested parties. Building work started early in 1879 and the Hospital was officially opened on 31st December 1880.

The cost of the building and furnishings of the Hospital amounted to £1500 and the first Matron received an annual salary of £30 plus board. Sadly, Dr Turner had passed away on 9th September 1877 but it was a fitting tribute to the late Practitioner that the Hospital was named 'The Turner Memorial Hospital', in memory of a hard-working Doctor with a vision.

DR ROBERT SHAND TURNER
1845 – 1931

Robert Shand Turner, son of Dr Robert Turner and Agnes (nee Kynoch), was born on 15th December 1845. He attended Keith Schools and in 1864 graduated MA from Aberdeen University. At Edinburgh he studied medicine and in 1867 graduated MB and CM He became a licentiate of the Royal College of Surgeons and worked in Edinburgh before joining his father's Keith practice, gaining a MD from Edinburgh a year later in 1870.

On his father's death in 1877, he took over the practice in which he remained serving the people of Keith and District until his retirement. He had been appointed Honorary Medical Superintendent of the newly-built Turner Memorial Hospital, where he had contributed his expertise and organising ability. The Kynoch Wards were added in 1893. He was Medical Officer of Health for Keith and for many years served as a Justice of the Peace for the County of Banff.

He was President of the Northern Counties Branch of the British Medical Association on several occasions and was the first President of Keith Grammar School Former Pupils' Association when it was formed in 1919. His service with the 6th Volunteer Battalion of the Gordon Highlanders saw him retiring as a Surgeon Lt. Colonel with a Volunteer Officers Decoration. Dr Turner and his wife resided at Craigduff, Seafield Avenue before retiring to Edinburgh. He died there on 25th June 1931.

SIR ROBERT URQUHART
1896 – 1983

Robert Urquhart was born in Forres in 1896 and spent his youth in Boharm at Mulben Station and at Calternach. He was educated at Boharm Primary School and from 1908 at Keith Grammar School.

In 1914 he went to Aberdeen University but had to interrupt his studies because of the outbreak of World War I. For the next four years he served in the Royal Navy as a telegraphist in the Adriatic, Aegean and Black Seas.

After the war he returned to Aberdeen University where he graduated MA in 1920 and then proceeded to Cambridge University for further studies before entering the Levant Consular Service as the sole British representative in the Smyrna Zone of Greek-occupied Turkey. In 1923 he was awarded the OBE and two years later married Brenda Phillips, daughter of a Professor at the Law School of the University of Cairo. He was later Vice Consul in Beruit and in 1934 was appointed Consul at Tabriz in Persia. From 1938 to 1942 he served in various capacities back in the UK, one of which was preparing to become the civilian administrator of Cornwall in the event of a German invasion of England. In 1942 he returned to Tabriz as Consul General, followed by a posting to New Orleans in 1943. He was awarded the CMG (Companion of St Michael and St George) in 1944 and became Inspector-General of Consular Establishments worldwide, This was followed by an appointment as British Minister in Washington D.C., then Consul General at Shanghai from 1948 to 1951 during which time he was knighted (KBE). In 1948 he predicted *"Nothing in the world can stop China from becoming a prosperous commercial and industrial power."* Note that George Jamieson, from Grange, held this prestigious post in the 1890's. (See page 74.)

While serving as British Ambassador in Venezuela (1951-1955), Sir Robert sent home money to establish a Club for Senior Citizens in Keith, which was called the Maracaibo Club after the Venezuelan city.

After his retirement from Government service, he became better known as Chairman of the Crofters Commission from 1955 to 1963.

In 1975 his wife died and in 1977 Sir Robert married Jane Gibson, an old friend from his Aberdeen college days.

Sir Robert Urquhart KBE, MA, LLD died in Edinburgh in 1983 aged 86 leaving a widow and four daughters.

Greece

Lebanon

Persia

Sir Robert Urquhart

Mulben Station

Maracaibo Club

Venezuela

U.S.A

China

P.R. China

Isla Bank Mills painting by John Tasker

Bridge of Isla Mills painting by John Tasker